EARTH SCIENCE

GW01080903

26

BOTTISHAM VILLAGE COLLEGE

Book Number .... **26** ....

Name	Form	Date Issued
J Br—		96
me	11.3	~~████~~
Yeah , you are good!	11 v2	97
Rebecca + Sam +	11th	'99
Leighanne	Yr.	4th March.

This book is on loan to you, and it is your
responsibility to look after it carefully.

Stanley Thornes (Publishers) Ltd

First published in 1992 by
Stanley Thornes (Publishers) Ltd
Old Station Drive
Leckhampton
CHELTENHAM   GL53 0DN

British Library Cataloguing in Publication Data

Bradberry, J.
    Earth science.
    I. Title
    551

    ISBN 0-7487-1280-1

Typeset by Tech-Set, Gateshead, Tyne & Wear.
Printed and bound in Great Britain by Ebenezer Baylis & Son, Worcester.

CONTENTS

Chapter 6   Water on the Land

Chapter 7   Earthquakes

Chapter 8   Continental Drift and Plate Movements

PREFACE

It is possible to think of the planet we live on as a huge vehicle travelling through space. This 'spaceship' supports and maintains all the life we see around us. It is important that we look after this Earth and attempt to understand it better. One step towards a better understanding and appreciation of our planet is to find out about the many processes involved in its formation.

This book is written to help you do just that. The Earth has a long history stretching back over 4000 million years. The work that earth scientists do is to look for evidence of the processes that have shaped the Earth, just as detectives look for clues to solve a crime. The clues are there in the environment around us – in the rocks, the soil, beaches, rivers and sky.

Many of the processes that helped to form the Earth as we know it today are still operating. For example, layers of rock are still being pushed into huge folds to form mountains as the continents slowly move.

Do you want to find out more? The key to any work in science is to be inquisitive. If you are curious about something and you work carefully to satisfy that curiosity, then you are well on the way to becoming a good scientist. If this book helps you to do this then the effort of writing it will be worthwhile.

As you work through the activities you will need to examine rock samples and other earth materials. In some cases you will be able to pick these up for yourself on fieldwork outings but you may need more specialist supplies, rock samples or equipment. Two recommended suppliers are Gregory Bottley & Lloyd, 8–12 Rickett Street, London SW6 1RH and Phillip Harris Education, Lynn Lane, Shenstone, Lichfield, Staffs WS14 0EE.

Finally my thanks go to my family and everyone who helped and advised me in the writing of this book. I hope you enjoy working with it as much as I have enjoyed writing it.

James Bradberry
Withywood School, Bristol
1992

ACKNOWLEDGEMENTS

The author and publishers are grateful to the following who gave permission for photographs or illustrations to be reproduced:

Associated Press 5.9, 7.1

British Geological Survey 4.6

Camera Press 2.1, 3.3

Casella London Limited 2.2, 6.10

Frank Spooner Pictures 3.7

G.S.F. Picture Library 3.1, 3.4, 5.5, 5.10

NASA 1.1

The Natural History Museum, London 4.1, 4.2, 4.3, 4.4, 4.7, 4.8, 4.9, 4.10, 4.13, 4.14, 4.15, 4.17, 4.20, 5.2, 8.1

The Times 2.9

THE PLANET EARTH

If you were on board an alien starship, how would your computer analyse this information about the third planet out from a star called Sun? Here is a possible simulation.

Figure 1.1 Earthrise from the Moon

EARTH

Diameter at Equator: 12 756 km

Orbital distance from star called Sun: 150 000 000 km

Planet surface: Water in liquid form, with ice-caps at the poles. No other planet in this system with so much water.

Atmosphere: nitrogen 78.09%
oxygen 20.95%
argon 0.93%
traces of other gases, including ozone, methane, carbon dioxide and water vapour 0.03%

Effects of the atmosphere (computer analysis):

a) Heat and climatic control:

The atmosphere moderates surface temperatures of the planet. Some heat from the Sun is trapped by the gases, in what Earthlings call the 'greenhouse effect'. This provides the right temperature range to maintain most of the Earth's water as a liquid. Water is only solid at the colder poles and on mountains.

Sensors show a recent increase in carbon dioxide due to Earthlings burning fuels. If this continues, the changed atmosphere will trap more of the Sun's heat, making the planet warmer.

The Sun heats the surface unevenly. There is more heat at the Equator than at the poles. Storms and air movements spread heat and moisture across the Earth's surface to produce different climatic conditions.

Figure 1.2 The Sun heats the Earth unevenly – why is it cooler at the poles?

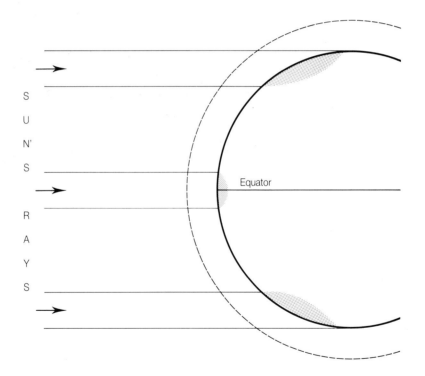

b) Shield protection:

Most objects pulled towards the planet such as meteors usually vaporise as they hit the atmosphere, so the gases act as a shield. An upper layer of oxygen in the atmosphere, known as O_3 (ozone), filters out Sun rays harmful to carbon-based life. Strangely, Earthlings are removing this gas from their 'shield' as they release harmful gases. Perhaps they do not realise this is happening.

c) Surface change:

Sensors show a varied landscape, with mountains, deep valleys and cliff-lines, unlike the cratered moonscape just behind us. Wind, rain, ice and rivers are attacking the surface rocks to make this scenery – this could not happen if there was no atmosphere.

Possibility of life:

The even temperatures and the presence of oxygen, carbon dioxide and water mean that this planet is the only one in this system likely to support life.

Recommendation:

Send down probe for closer observation of the surface.

EXERCISE 1

The Earth's atmosphere

1) Construct a pie-chart to show the composition of the atmosphere.

2) How would you describe the amount of water vapour and carbon dioxide in the Earth's atmosphere?

3) How does the atmosphere control the Sun's heat?

4) What is the 'greenhouse effect'?

5) Make your own copy of Figure 1.2 and show where most and least heat is received. Explain the reasons for this.

6) Explain the two main ways in which the atmosphere shields the Earth. *Because the USA use it as a nuclear testing site, hence no*

7) Why does the Moon appear so heavily cratered when *Life*. the Earth does not?

8) What factors made the Earth so favourable to the development of life?

9) Write out these sentences, selecting the correct alternative.
   (a) The Earth's atmosphere is mainly composed of (oxygen/nitrogen).
   (b) The atmosphere moderates extremes of (temperature/radiation).
   (c) Atmospheric (ozone/carbon dioxide) filters out harmful solar radiation.
   (d) Hot air rises at the (equator/poles) and cold air sinks at the (equator/poles) to create a global (wind/circulation) of air.

10) For each pair of statements, write down the one you think is the most accurate:

(a) The atmosphere burns up unwanted meteors, before they hit the surface.
    Most meteors break up and melt, before they hit the surface.

(b) The greenhouse effect is beneficial because without it the Earth would be a very cold planet.
    The greenhouse effect is harmful because it is mainly caused by humans polluting the atmosphere.

ACTIVITY 1

What would the Earth be like with no atmosphere?

Draw a poster of what the Earth's landscapes might look like if there were no atmosphere. Decide what items to sketch in – would you show oceans, lakes, rivers, cliffs, mountains, meteor craters, volcanoes? Make notes, giving reasons for your decisions.

EARTH HISTORY

How the Earth began

The Sun and the planets surrounding it were very different 5000 million years ago. At that time there was a huge cold cloud of gas and dust in space, called a *nebula* (see Figure 1.3). This broke up to form a large central 'cloud' which, in time, condensed and contracted in size to become the Sun. Surrounding it there were smaller 'clouds'. The gas and dust in these 'clouds' also began to condense to form the planets. Larger planets were able to hold lighter gases by their stronger gravity and keep an atmosphere, but the smaller planets were not able to do so.

Figure 1.3 Four stages in the evolution of the Solar System from a nebula

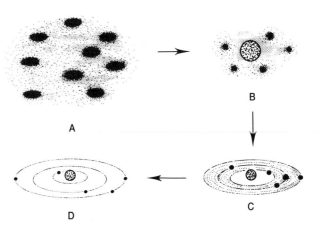

What was the early Earth like?

The Earth, 4500 million years ago, was not a particularly pleasant place. At first, the Earth might have looked something like Jupiter does today, with a thick atmosphere of light gases. As the Sun started to radiate sunlight much of this atmosphere was forced away into space. At that time, most of the Earth was molten, with many more volcanoes than there are today. The volcanoes produced an atmosphere of water vapour, nitrogen, ammonia, carbon monoxide, carbon dioxide and methane.

EXERCISE 2

The early Earth

Discuss these questions in groups and compare your answers.

1) Why would the gases mentioned above be lost from Earth but not from Jupiter?

2) At this stage, would there have been any surface water?

3) What must have happened to surface temperatures before rain could fall?

Where the seas came from

As time passed, enough surface water collected for shallow seas to form, and the first simple plants began to evolve. The water gave some protection from the Sun's deadly ultraviolet radiation, giving a moderate environment where temperatures did not vary so much.

How the atmosphere began to change

As green plants began to flourish in the seas, they were able to turn water and carbon dioxide into simple foods and oxygen. They still do this, using energy from sunlight.

Formation of the ozone layer

In time, the Sun's ultraviolet radiation turned some oxygen in the upper atmosphere to ozone. This formed a protective layer screening out the Sun's harmful rays. Life was able to develop faster and animals appeared in the water. Shallow water plants began to colonise swamps and developed new root systems for life on land. Land animals then appeared, taking advantage of the new food sources.

Changes in the early atmosphere

1) Copy Figure 1.4, drawing in line graphs for carbon dioxide and oxygen, using the information given in the table below.

Millions of years ago	Carbon dioxide (percentage composition)	Oxygen (percentage composition)
4500	90	0
4000	40	0
3500	21	traces
3000	15	1
2500	10	5
2000	7	10
1500	5	18
1000	2	22
500	1	24
0	less than 1	24

2) Give two reasons why the amounts of carbon dioxide decreased with time.

3) Why did the amount of oxygen increase with time?

4) Why were the new oceans safe places for life to evolve?

5) What event made it possible for life to evolve more freely?

Figure 1.4 Changes in the composition of the atmosphere through time

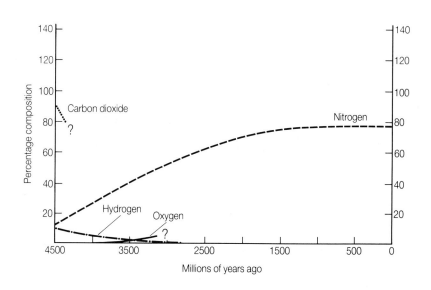

The age of the Earth

Figure 1.5 shows the main events in Earth history. Use this timescale to answer the following questions.

Figure 1.5 The time-scale of the Earth

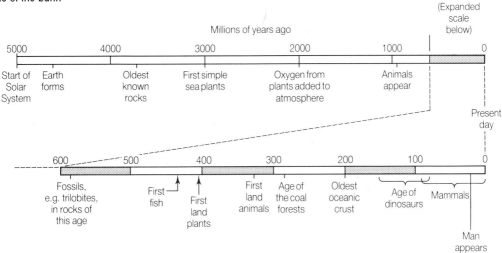

1) When did land plants first appear?

2) Explain why there were no animals before 1000 million years ago.

3) Here is a list of some of the Earth's main events. Write the list in correct chronological (time) order (starting with the earliest event).

- The first land plants
- The first land animals
- The first simple sea plants
- The first sea animals

4) Stretch some string across the classroom and mark off the timescale in millions of years. Then attach pegged labels to your scale to show the position of the main events.

THE EARTH'S STRUCTURE

What is the Earth like inside?

Imagine that you hijack one of the Channel Tunnel rock boring machines and adapt it for a journey to the centre of the Earth. The following paragraphs tell you what the inside of the Earth is like – when you have read them and studied Figure 1.6 (overleaf), write an essay on your journey, giving the thickness of each layer you pass through.

Figure 1.6 The Earth's structure (the scale is in thousands of kilometres)

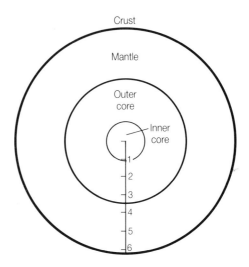

The inner core

Rocks deep inside the Earth are under very high pressures and temperatures. The temperature at the centre of the Earth is 3500 °C, yet the inner core remains solid because of the great pressures – 3 million times surface pressure. The core is a mixture of iron and nickel with sulphur, at a high density, with 10 grams packed into one cubic centimetre, i.e. 10 g/cm^3. (For comparison, the density of surface water is 1 g/cm^3.)

The outer core

The outer core has the same composition and temperature as the inner core, but because the pressure is slightly less, it is a liquid layer. Swirling movements within the outer core set up electromagnetic currents which give the Earth a strong magnetic field. The field behaves much like a bar magnet, to give a north–south polarity (see Figure 1.7).

ACTIVITY 2

Testing the Earth's magnetism

- Rub a needle with a bar magnet, then float it on water in the middle of a shallow dish. Compare its movement with that of an unmagnetised needle and of a magnetic compass needle. Explain fully what you find out.
- Sprinkle iron filings on paper above a bar magnet. What happens to the filings when you tap the paper? How does the pattern compare to Figure 1.7?

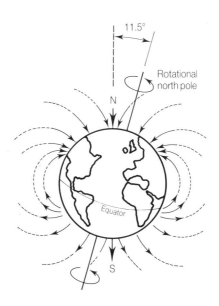

Figure 1.7 The Earth's magnetic field

The mantle

The mantle is a solid rock layer, with an average density of 4.5 g/cm³. The mantle behaves as a plastic solid, allowing very slow movements called *convection currents*, to take place. Hot rocks flow slowly towards the surface where they cause pockets of very hot rock just below the surface. Some melting may occur and *magma* (molten rock) may cause surface volcanoes.

ACTIVITY 3

Investigating convection

Allow some crystals of potassium permanganate to drop down a hollow tube to the bottom of a beaker full of cold water (see Figure 1.8). Then gently heat the water.

- What happens as the water is heated?
- Sketch the movement that takes place – how might it compare with what happens in the mantle?

Figure 1.8 Convection currents

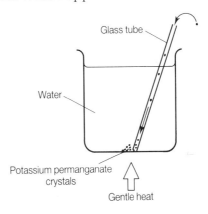

Oceanic and continental crust

The crust is a thin layer of surface rocks, with a density of about 2.8 g/cm³. There are two different types of crust (see Figure 1.9). Oceanic crust is found beneath all oceans and covers 65% of the Earth's surface. It is only 8 km thick and is mostly composed of a rock called basalt, which has formed from mantle magma at some time in the last 200 million years. Continental crust is 35 km thick on average and is made up of all kinds of different rocks. They have been folded by many earth movements over millions of years and are generally older than oceanic crustal rocks.

Figure 1.9 The two types of crust (density values are shown in g/cm³)

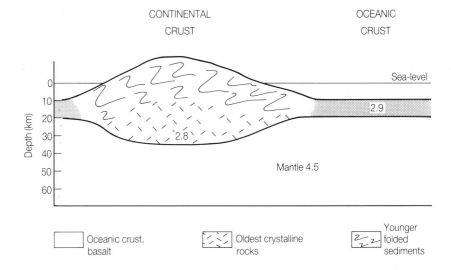

The continents behave like blocks of ice floating on water. They cannot sink into the mantle because their density is so

The age of the Earth's crust

Refer back to Figure 1.5 on page 7 and use the timescale which you made for Exercise 4.

1) Mark the earliest date for oceanic crust on your timescale. Has oceanic crust formed quickly or slowly, compared to the Earth's total age?

2) Is continental crust older or younger than oceanic crust?

3) Check where the oldest rock is on your classroom timescale. Roughly how many times older is it than oceanic crust?

Density considerations

The continents behave like blocks of ice floating on water. They cannot sink into the mantle because their density is so low. Their buoyancy is the main reason continental masses have survived destruction despite years of erosion. On the other hand, oceanic crust is more dense and eventually it returns to the mantle (you will find out more about this in Chapter 8).

ACTIVITY 4

Continents and erosion

- To represent rocks on a continental mass, place a slab of Plasticine on top of a wedge of wood and float the wood in water as shown in Figure 1.10.
- Mark the waterline with a waterproof felt pen.
- To represent erosion, remove the Plasticine and refloat the wood – what happens to the waterline? Why?
- Sketch both stages of this activity.
- In the last ice age there was a huge thickness of ice in northern Europe – what effect do you think this had on the level of the continent?
- Ten thousand years ago the ice sheets melted as the climate became warmer – what do you think has happened to the level of the European continent since then?

Figure 1.10 Floating a model of a continent

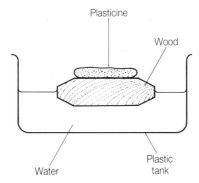

QUESTIONS ON CHAPTER 1

1 Write out and complete the following sentences about the Earth, using the words listed below.

magnetic   convection   nickel

continental   liquid   iron

(a) The central core is a mixture of ___ and ___ with sulphur.
(b) The outer core is the only completely ___ layer inside the Earth.

(c) Swirling movements in the outer core cause the ___ field.

(d) ___ currents are present in the mantle.

(e) The oldest crust is ___.

2 Make an accurate scaled sketch of the Earth's structure, based on Figure 1.6 on page 8.

3 Tabulate the main differences between oceanic and continental crust.

THE WEATHER

In January 1990 there were severe gales in much of Britain. Eighteen people were killed and many houses and schools were damaged.

Figure 2.1 The storms blew trees down, causing widespread damage

EXERCISE 1

Effects and uses of wind

1) Prepare a report for your local paper on the effects of a bad storm.

2) Winds are not always harmful -- make a list of the uses of wind.

MEASURING WIND

Winds help to control the weather we experience. The destructiveness of storms is caused by strong winds, so it is useful to make measurements of wind force to find out if wind speeds are increasing or decreasing. In the early days of sailing ships there were no instruments for measuring wind but, in 1805, Admiral Francis Beaufort overcame this problem by devising a wind scale (0 = calm to 12 = hurricane). This was used by sailors to assess the wind and to set the right amount of sail on their ships.

ACTIVITY 1

Devise your own wind scale

- Watch the effects of wind blowing on smoke, kites, litter, drying clothes etc. Then make your own six-point wind scale, based on what you have observed.

Wind strength	Effects of the wind
Calm	
Slight breeze	
Moderate breeze	
Strong breeze	
Gale	
Storm	

- Decide what your wind scale number for each of the following events would be:
  — large tree branches moving
  — some tiles being blown off the roof of a house
  — a caravan being overturned
  — a furniture van being blown off the motorway
  — crisp packets being blown out of litter bins
  — a car being smashed by a falling tree
  — a boy being blown off his bicycle.

- Make a poster version of your wind scale, with a picture for each of the wind descriptions.
- An amateur yachtsman is about to sail into the Bristol channel. He hears this message on the weather forecast at 12 noon: 'force 9 gale slowly moderating to force 6 by 1800 hours ...'. What does this message mean? When would it be safe for him to leave harbour?

RECORDING THE WIND

Wind speed is measured using an *anemometer* (see Figure 2.2). The cups spin as they are caught by the wind and the rate of spin is recorded in kilometres per hour (km/h).

ACTIVITY 2

Making an anemometer and a wind vane

- Design an anemometer to measure the speed of the wind. You could base this on Figure 2.2 or use a different design.

- A *wind vane* records the direction the wind is coming from (see Figure 2.2). Design and make a wind vane. You will need a freely rotating pointer, flat enough to catch the wind, and a compass to work out directions.
- Use the two instruments you have made to keep a daily record of wind speed and direction. What patterns can you see in your records over a fortnight?
- One way to record this information is on a wind rose chart (see Figure 2.3). Draw a line each day along the correct direction arm of the rose and write in the wind speed.

Figure 2.2 A wind vane and an anemometer

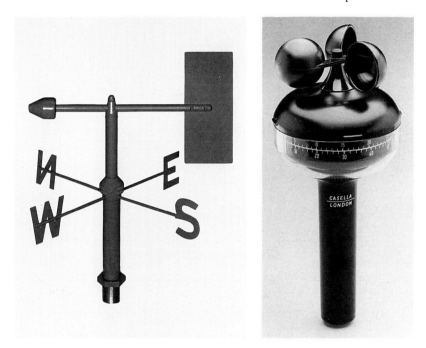

Figure 2.3 A wind rose chart

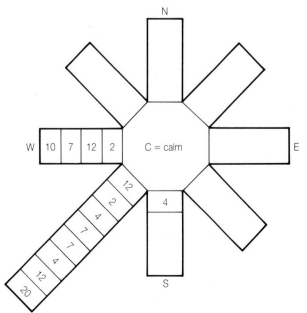

WEATHER CHANGES

The wind direction is often linked with the kind of weather we experience.

ACTIVITY 3

Wind direction and weather

- Make some long-term observations to find out the usual weather for the following wind directions in winter and summer.

Wind direction	Usual weather
Easterly	
Northerly	
Westerly	
Southerly	

- Summarise your findings on an outline map of the British Isles.

Weather is not only about the effects of wind, but is concerned with every tiny change in the Earth's atmosphere.

ACTIVITY 4

Changes in the weather

- Make your own word search puzzle about the weather. List the words you include below the puzzle. Here are a few words to get you started:

  fog   frost   rain   snow   temperature   sunshine ...

- List the main instruments and methods which are used to record changes in the weather.
- Choose one of the instruments you have listed and use it to investigate the weather over several days, near your home or school.
- Compare your results with data collected by other people.
- Display your results – for example, rainfall figures can be shown on a bar graph and temperature changes on a line graph.

WHAT IS AIR PRESSURE?

Although air is invisible, it has mass and is pushing downwards. This is called atmospheric pressure. There is about 1 kg of air pressing down on each square centimetre of the Earth's surface. We don't collapse under this pressure because the fluid pressure inside our bodies balances it.

Does air have mass?

- Weigh a deflated balloon using a top-pan balance.
- Inflate the balloon and reweigh it.
- Record and explain your results.

Pressure on you

- Place your hand on a sheet of graph paper and draw an outline.
- Calculate the total area of your hand in square centimetres.
- What is the mass of the atmosphere pressing down on your hand?

WHAT THE ATMOSPHERE IS LIKE

Figure 2.4 shows the structure of the atmosphere, based on information from balloons carrying instruments. Eighty per cent of all the air is within the troposphere, together with nearly all the water vapour. All the winds, rain and other types of weather occur here.

Figure 2.4 The atmosphere

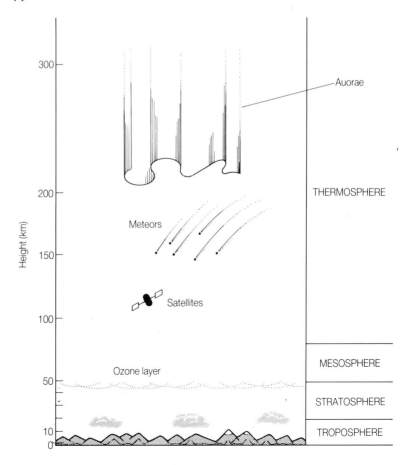

The highest cirrus clouds of ice crystals are found at 50 km above the Earth's surface, at the top of the stratosphere, where the weather is otherwise clear. Many passenger jets fly at this level.

In the highest layers of the atmosphere (the mesosphere and thermosphere) the air is thin, but there is enough air resistance to make meteors glow and disintegrate because of frictional heat. Radiation from the Sun causes disturbances, creating charged particles in glowing curtains of light called aurorae.

How winds circulate

The Earth's swirling cloud patterns are evidence of the global circulating air system. Air movements are kept going by energy from the Sun. Surface air is heated in tropical regions, where it expands and rises, cooling as it moves north and south over colder regions, to eventually sink at the poles.

<table>
<tr><td>ACTIVITY 7</td><td></td></tr>
</table>

Cold air and warm air – which is heavier?

- Set up two flasks as shown in Figure 2.5, so that they are in balance.
- What happens when you gently heat one of the flasks?
- Allow the flask to cool – how do the flasks move during the cooling process?
- What happens if you now heat the other flask?
- Make a series of labelled sketches of the flasks to show what happens, labelling the directions of movement.
- Which is heavier – cold or warm air?

Figure 2.5 Which is heavier – warm or cold air?

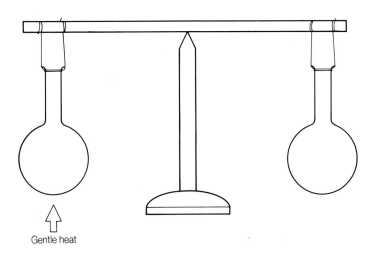

Gentle heat

Does air expand when heated?

- Stretch a rubber balloon over the end of a test-tube.
- Gently heat the test-tube, by placing it in hot water. Explain what happens.

WHY DOES AIR MOVE?

- How and why do small pieces of tissue paper move above a radiator?
- What is this process called? There is a clue in Chapter 1, Activity 3.

Where air is rising, the atmosphere is not so dense and has less mass, so atmospheric pressure is lower than normal. Cooler heavier air sinks to take its place. A circulating convection cell is set up. Beneath sinking air, atmospheric pressure is higher than normal.

Land and sea breezes

One of the best examples of a convection cell can often be observed at the seaside, where the land and sea react differently to the Sun's heat. Figure 2.6 shows what happens.

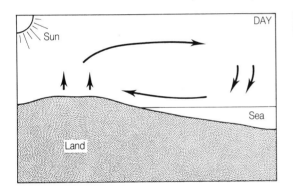
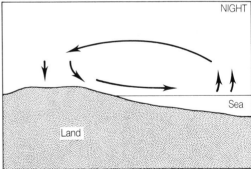

Figure 2.6 Local onshore and offshore breezes

1) During the day, which will heat up the quickest – air just above the land or above the sea?

2) At night, which will cool the quickest – the land or the sea?

3) Why are temperatures at the seaside on a hot day often several degrees lower than those inland?

4) If you were walking along the beach on a sunny day which way would the wind be blowing?

5) Which way would the wind be blowing on the same beach at night?

6) Fully explain what is happening in both parts of Figure 2.6.

7) Make a copy of Figure 2.6 and label the areas where pressure would be 'high' and 'low'. Give reasons for your answer.

THE GLOBAL CIRCULATION

Figure 2.6 shows a local circulation between land and sea – what might the global pattern be between the equator and the poles? In the eighteenth century, George Hadley realised air was rising at the equator and flowing north and south to sink at the poles.

- Why would he have thought this?

He had the right idea but the distance from the equator to the poles is over 10 000 km. Air cools and sinks long before it reaches the poles. What really happens is shown in Figure 2.7.

- How many convection cells can you see?

Figure 2.7 Global convection cells

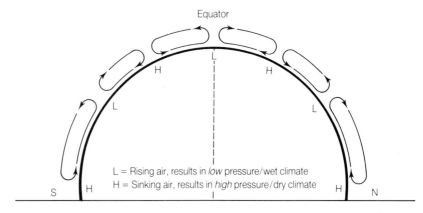

L = Rising air, results in *low* pressure/wet climate
H = Sinking air, results in *high* pressure/dry climate

The effect of land and sea

In summer, air over the continents becomes warmer than over the oceans. This happens in the Indian monsoon (see Figure 2.8). In summer the central plains of India are heated and air rises.

1) Would this create a high or low pressure zone?

2) Moist cool air from over the ocean is drawn in and is forced to rise over warmer air inland – what kind of weather would you expect this to produce?

Figure 2.8 The Indian monsoon (arrows show air movements)

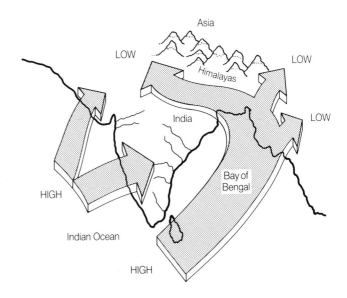

3) The opposite effect occurs in winter when the air over the sea is warmer than the air over the land. Then the wind blows the other way – would you expect this to be India's wet or dry season? Give your reasons.

4) Draw labelled maps to show what is happening in summer and in winter. Show wind directions and where areas of high and low pressure would develop.

High and low pressure

Figure 2.9 shows a newspaper weather chart. The lines which circle the areas of high and low pressure, known as isobars, join together places of equal pressure, which is measured in millibars. Winds always blow from high to low pressure.

Figure 2.9 A newspaper weather map, 1 March 1991 (source: *The Times*)

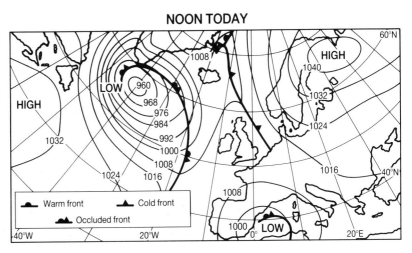

21

1) How many areas of high and low pressure are shown on the map?

2) The closer together the isobars, the stronger the winds. Would you associate strong winds with high or low pressure?

3) Low-pressure areas are sometimes called depressions – why is this?

4) Copy the map and mark on it where pressure is lowest/highest.

5) On your map, use big arrows to show where the winds will be very strong and small arrows to show where the winds will be light. (Winds blow clockwise around 'highs' and anti-clockwise around 'lows' in the northern hemisphere).

6) What are the thicker lines that are shown on the map called?

AIR MOVEMENTS AND WEATHER

As air moves from high to low pressure, warm moist air is forced to rise in a spiral over colder denser air within a depression. Air expands as it rises because it is under less pressure. This causes sudden cooling and water vapour condenses to form cloud and rain. By contrast, the gently sinking air in an anticyclone is contracting. The air is warming up, so there is little condensation, cloud or rain.

Fronts

Over the mid-Atlantic, warm tropical air moving north meets cold air from the Arctic moving south, at a line called a front. The two kinds of air do not mix easily. Warm air has less mass and tends to rise, whereas cold air is heavy and tends to sink. A whirlpool of air movement develops as warm air spirals up over the cold air. The sloping boundary between the two kinds of air is the line of the warm front. The cold air behind pushes under the warm air to form the line of the cold front (see Figure 2.10). Mid-Atlantic storms which form in this way often move across Britain.

Figure 2.10 A
developing front
system

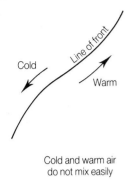

Cold

Line of front

Warm

Cold and warm air
do not mix easily

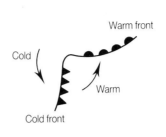

Warm front

Cold

Warm

Cold front

Warm air spirals
up over cold air

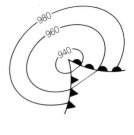

980
960
940

Uprush of warm air
creates a low-pressure cell

EXERCISE 5

Depressions and anticyclones

1) Write out the following statements inserting the correct words.

   In a depression the air is sinking/rising. The pressure is high/low. Air is expanding/contracting. The air is wet/dry. The weather produced is usually fine/dull.

2) Describe how air behaves in an anticyclone.

Occlusions

In a depression, cold fronts move faster than warm fronts and catch them up. Eventually the warm air is lifted up completely and an occluded front is formed (see Figure 2.11).

Figure 2.11 An
occluded front

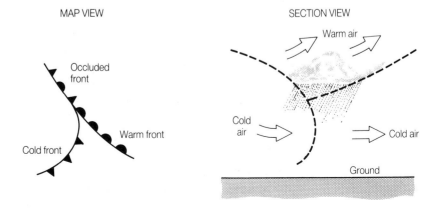

MAP VIEW

Occluded front

Cold front

Warm front

SECTION VIEW

Warm air

Cold air

Cold air

Ground

The passage of a depression

Study the cross-section shown in Figure 2.12.

Figure 2.12 Side view
of the passage of a
depression

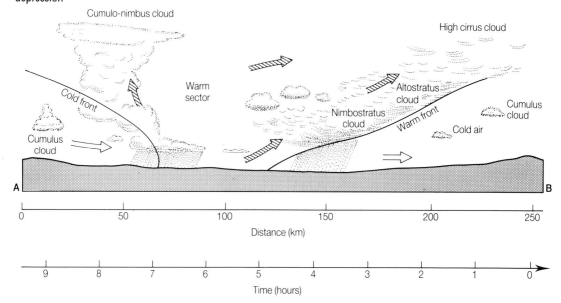

1) How wide is the storm from A to B, and in what direction is it moving?

2) What was the time interval between the appearance of cirrus cloud and the first drops of rain?

3) How could the clouds be used to forecast the weather?

4) You have decided to have a picnic, but there is an approaching warm and cold front. Write a log of the weather each hour.

5) A rain gauge (see Figure 6.10 on page 81) was used to record the amount of rainfall every hour as a warm and cold front passed over. Make a bar graph to show the results given in the table below.

Time	Rainfall
4–5 a.m.	2 mm
5–6 a.m.	8 mm
6–7 a.m.	14 mm
7–8 a.m.	21 mm
8–9 a.m.	2 mm
9–10 a.m.	1 mm
11–12 noon	8 mm
1–2 p.m.	3 mm

6) How much rain fell in the wettest hour?

7) Label on your bar graph when the warm and cold fronts passed over.

8) Use a rain gauge to make your own records of the passage of a storm.

CLIMATE

Dry summers and snowy winters are unusual kinds of weather in Britain. It is more normal for us to have showery weather for much of the year. Why is this? The pattern of weather over several years is known as the 'average weather' or climate. This pattern can be seen in annual records of temperature, pressure and rainfall. The table below shows the average rainfall (in millimetres) for the British Isles.

J	F	M	A	M	J	J	A	S	O	N	D
92	66	57	60	63	55	79	81	76	92	95	88

Each monthly total is calculated by adding the rainfall totals for that month over 35 years, then dividing by 35.

EXERCISE 7

Britain's climate

1) Make a bar graph using the average rainfall figures shown in the table above.

2) Which are the wettest and driest months?

3) What is the total annual rainfall?

4) Calculate the average monthly rainfall. How many months have a rainfall figure above and how many below this average?

5) Complete the statement below in the most accurate way.

    On average, Britain's climate is ...
    • very cold and damp
    • dry and cool most of the year
    • mild and wet throughout the year
    • wet in winter, drier in spring/early summer.

QUESTIONS ON CHAPTER 2

1 'Very wet windy conditions are common in low pressure systems.' Explain what this statement means.

2 What are the main differences between warm, cold and occluded fronts?

3 Look at Figure 2.9 on page 21 and describe what you think the weather would be like in Spain, France and Britain.

4 Based on Figure 2.9, what would your forecast be for the weather in Iceland the following day, given that the low is moving north-east?

5 Look at the weather forecast in a newspaper. Then write down the actual weather – how accurate was the forecast?

6 Give examples of extremes of British weather that do not follow the pattern of a normal British climate.

7 Make a climate graph to show the following figures for Kew, England.

Month	J	F	M	A	M	J	J	A	S	O	N	D
Temperature (°C)	5	6	8	10	13	15	18	17	16	10	7	5
Rainfall (mm)	45	36	26	45	46	25	54	52	50	53	56	51

Compare your graph with the graphs for a hot desert climate and a tropical climate, as shown in a good atlas.

CHAPTER

3

VOLCANOES

Most volcanoes are formed by the accumulation of layers of material that have been forced out of a hole or a crack in the Earth's surface, in events called eruptions. Most volcanoes are cone-shaped mountains because the material piles up near the vent (see Figure 3.1).

Figure 3.1 Teide volcano, Tenerife

Eruptions are often spectacular and hazardous events. Magma reaches the surface as molten lava and droplets of it are often blasted into the sky, along with hot clouds of powdered rock called ash. When Mt Pelée erupted on the island of Martinique in 1902, a suffocating cloud of ash reached a height of 24 km and spread sideways to flatten trees 25 km away. Almost all of the 30 000 people in the nearby town of San Pierre lost their lives.

IS IT REALLY ASH?

The clouds of so-called 'ash' mixed with water vapour, suggest that a burning process must take place in volcanoes. In fact there is no combustion at all and the only smoke that you might see would be from trees set alight by the lava.

MUDFLOWS

Sometimes the heat will melt snow and ice on the summit of a volcano. Water mixes with the ash to form mudflows capable of moving at 80 km/hour. In the 1985 eruption of the volcano Nevada del Ruiz in Columbia, a huge river of mud flowed downhill, burying 23 000 people in the town of Armero.

WHY LIVE NEAR VOLCANOES?

The slopes of volcanoes are attractive places for farmers to live and work because as old layers of ash and lava slowly break down by the action of the weather, fertile soils are often formed and crops grow well. People may believe the volcano they live on is extinct – in fact volcanoes can be dormant (inactive) for thousands of years before suddenly erupting again.

EXERCISE 1

Studying pressures and temperatures

Volcanoes give clues to high pressures and temperatures that can exist near the Earth's surface.

1) What evidence of high pressures and temperatures is mentioned in the first paragraphs of this chapter?

2) Colour can be a guide to temperature, as shown by the table below:

Colour	Temperature (°C)
white	above 1150
yellow	900–1150
red	500–900

Using this table, estimate the temperature of the following:
- the heated element of a toaster
- the filament of a light bulb.

3) Decide what temperature the lava is in the picture on the front cover.

4) How many times greater than the boiling point of water is this temperature?

5) Why is it that farmers who lived on the slopes of a volcano might be unable to return to their land for many years after an eruption?

THE CASE OF HEIMAEY

Heimaey is a quiet island to the south of Iceland (see Figure 3.2). In 1973, its 5000 inhabitants mainly earned a living from sea fishing and processing. The volcano they lived on had not erupted for 7000 years. Then one night, when most of the fishing boats were in harbour, the volcano split open and clouds of ash and lava fountains erupted from a crack near the summit. Huge amounts of black ash were blown on to the roofs of buildings causing their collapse. For four months the islanders swept the ash off their roofs and bulldozed it from their streets (see Figure 3.3). They also sprayed millions of gallons of seawater on to the lava flow as it approached the town. This slowed the lava down. Most of the lava flowed towards the harbour and for a time, it looked as though the harbour would be completely destroyed. Finally the eruption ceased. Now the people live on a bigger island and they have free hot water from pipes that they have buried in the cooling lava flows. The cindery ash has been used to make a new runway for the airfield.

Figure 3.2 Heimaey Island

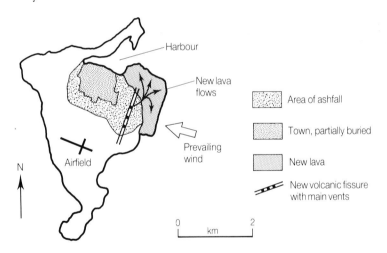

Figure 3.3 Ash in the streets

Looking at the Heimaey eruption

1) On the night of the eruption the town had to be evacuated in a hurry.
   (a) Why was it impossible to use aircraft to do this?
   (b) What method do you think the islanders used?

2) Study the sketch map in Figure 3.2.
   (a) Why did the ash mainly fall to the west of the volcanic fissure?
   (b) Draw a sketch map to show what might have happened if the lava had advanced across the harbour mouth.

3) When the eruption stopped and the islanders tried to grow crops again, they discovered a problem with salt in the soil. Why?

4) The islanders put pipes into the cooling lava – why did they do this? Write some notes on how they might have solved the technical problems.

5) Does it surprise you that people are still getting hot water from the pipes in the lava 20 years after the eruption? Make a side view sketch of a lava flow and label where you think the rocks would be coolest and hottest, showing where you would bury the water pipes. Give your reasons.

6) The ash and lava caused damage but there were some benefits, such as 'free' hot water. Write down two other benefits for the islanders.

THE CAUSES OF ERUPTIONS

Volcanoes vary greatly in their behaviour. Before an eruption, gas pressure increases beneath the volcano. The more explosive volcanoes produce more ash because the pressure is greater and pulverises more rock. Explosions clear the blocked vent of rocks. The fine ash rock erupts from the volcano in a hot dense cloud.

CAN VOLCANOES AFFECT WORLD CLIMATE?

The ash may settle on the slopes of the volcano or winds may carry it hundreds of kilometres before it settles. In the 1883 Krakatoa eruption, a volcanic island blew up and threw ash 80 km into the sky, where it remained suspended for several years, blocking out some of the Sun's heat. This caused a series of poor summers and cold winters throughout the world.

WHY IS LAVA ERUPTED?

In an eruption, once the surface vent is clear, lava is frequently erupted. This happens in much the same way as a fizzy drink foaming out of a bottle with the top removed. As the vent is unblocked, the sudden release of pressure causes dissolved gases in the magma to expand and push out the molten rock. Pumice is frothy lava that has cooled and hardened. It is so full of gas bubbles that it will float in seawater.

ACTIVITY 1

Investigating pumice

- Try submerging a piece of pumice in water – what happens?
- Examine a sample of pumice, using a hand lens. Sketch the bubble structure.
- Find out what happens to carbonated water as it degasses from a bottle on removal of the top – how does this show what happens in a volcano?

DIFFERENT KINDS OF LAVA

When a lava flow cools it may have a ropy twisted texture on its upper surface, or a blocky cindery texture (see Figure 3.4). The texture will depend on the temperature and chemistry of the lava, as shown in the table below.

Ropy lava	Blocky lava
Temperature 1000 °C	Temperature 700 °C
Low silica content	High silica content
Flows easily	Thick, treacly, slow-flowing

Figure 3.4 Ropy and blocky lava, Hawaii

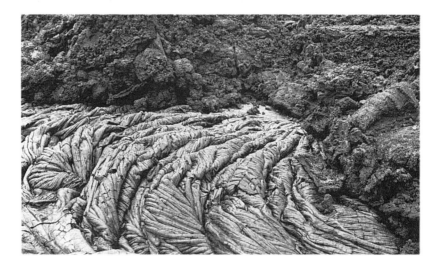

When lava is thick and pasty it blocks the vent, causing a build-up of gas pressure and consequently more explosions. In the Mt St Helens eruption in the USA in 1980, the top half of the mountain exploded and a heavy ash cloud rolled down the mountainside, killing 60 people and destroying everything in its path. Trees were flattened like stalks of corn over an area of 500 km².

The world's largest volcano, called Mauna Loa, rises from the sea-bed of the Pacific Ocean. Its summit forms the island of Hawaii (see Figure 3.5). Here the lava is very runny and flows a long distance from the vent. A large shallow sloping cone has built up to form a shield volcano.

- What is its diameter?

Figure 3.5 Main island, Hawaii

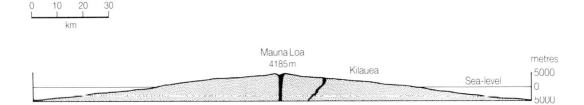

EXERCISE 3

Studying lava types

1) Which lava type would form fast-flowing rivers down a slope in an eruption?

2) Make a labelled sketch of blocky and ropy lava based on Figure 3.4 – which is which? Give your reasons.

3) Which kind of lava would pose the greatest threat to life? Give reasons.

4) Figure 3.6 shows side-views of two volcanoes.

Figure 3.6 Two types of volcano

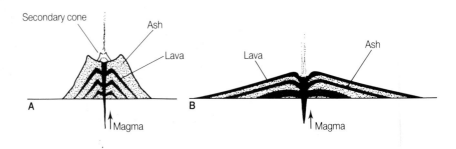

(a) Which of these volcanoes is likely to produce free-flowing lava and which is likely to produce thick lava? Why?

(b) Which of these volcanoes would be the more explosive and which would be the less explosive? Say why.

5) What is the height of Mauna Loa in metres: (a) from the sea-bed, and (b) from sea-level?

6) How wide is the base of Mauna Loa beneath the sea?

7) The largest volcano ever found is Olympus Mons on the planet Mars. It is 23 km high and has a base diameter of 500 km. Compare the relative sizes of Mauna Loa and Olympus Mons by drawing scaled sketches of these two volcanoes.

VOLCANIC GASES

The most common volcanic gases are water vapour, carbon dioxide and sulphur dioxide. Over millions of years, volcanoes have helped to change the Earth's atmosphere. They have steadily added more water and carbon dioxide to the atmosphere and oceans.

There are several examples of volcanic gases causing deaths. In 1986, at Lake Nyos in Cameroon, 1700 lakeside villagers and many of their livestock were killed when a deadly cloud of carbon dioxide gas burst out of the lake and choked them to death (see Figure 3.7). Carbon dioxide is a heavy gas and it will collect in hollows and valleys where it pushes away the other gases including oxygen. In the Lake Nyos case, the gas seeped out from the volcano into the lower waters of the lake over a period of 20 years before the eruption. Surviving villagers have been warned to beware of a similar event happening again.

Figure 3.7 Eruption of carbon dioxide at Lake Nyos, Cameroon

Investigating the effects of CO₂

Place a lighted candle at the bottom of a beaker. Fill a flask with CO_2. Pour the gas down a paper gutter into the beaker. What happens to the lighted flame? Why does this happen?

Threats from volcanoes

1) In the case of Lake Nyos, what field observations would you make to find out about the gas build-up?

2) From the information given on the previous page, how many years from now would you warn the villagers to evacuate the area?

3) From what you have read so far, make a list of the different ways in which volcanic activity threatens peoples lives – rank them from the most to the least hazardous.

4) Is it safer to live on a volcano like Mauna Loa or a volcano like Mt St Helens? Give your reasons.

WHERE ARE THEY ALL?

There are about 500 recently active volcanoes in the world, but only about 20 of them are likely to erupt in any one year. In this context, 'recently' means any time in the last 10 000 years. The distribution of volcanoes is shown in Figure 3.8.

Figure 3.8 The world's volcanoes

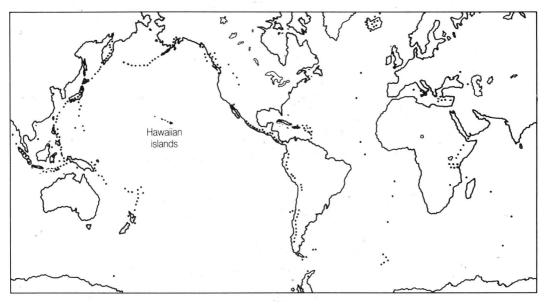

Note that they are not scattered randomly, but mostly lie in long narrow chains. In most cases the sites of volcanoes coincide with the positions of the world's earthquakes and fold mountains (see the maps on pages 86 and 98).

Active and stable zones

The pattern of volcanoes, earthquakes and fold mountains occurring in narrow linear belts suggests that there are 'active zones' where there is heat and movement. Away from these zones the Earth's surface is stable with far less heat and activity. The reasons for this are explained later, in Chapter 8.

EXERCISE 5

Locations of volcanoes

1) Here are some statements about the distribution of the world's volcanoes. Decide which are true and which are false and write out any true statements.
   - Nearly all volcanoes are near the sea.
   - There are few volcanoes in the centres of continents.
   - There are few active volcanoes in the British Isles.
   - There is a line of volcanoes right round the Pacific Ocean.
   - There is a line of volcanoes right round the Atlantic Ocean.
   - In the mid-Atlantic, there is a line of volcanoes from Iceland to Antarctica.
   - There are no volcanoes in very cold countries.

FORECASTING ERUPTIONS

The best way to predict an eruption is to watch a volcano carefully. Given that there are 500 volcanoes throughout the world that need watching, this could be an impossible task. A better way is to use routine infra-red satellite photos and see if any of the world's dormant volcanoes are beginning to heat up. If they are, then ground equipment can be moved in to monitor the changes more closely.

Tiltmeters

Many volcanoes swell slightly before they begin to erupt, as the magma moves upwards. Changes in slope are measured with a kind of spirit-level called a tiltmeter. The difficulty is saying exactly when a volcano will erupt – the slow swelling of the summit can be as little as 1 m in 10 years!

Seismometers

A seismometer is an instrument which is very sensitive to vibrations. As magma begins to move, many small earthquakes are recorded. Just before an eruption, there could be as many as 1000 minor shallow earthquakes a day.

Gas sensors

Gas sensors detect changes in escaping gases. More gas is likely to escape if the magma is close to the surface.

The magnetic properties of rocks also change when they are heated. If all these methods are used, then an eruption can be predicted. The difficulty is in knowing the exact day on which it will happen.

INTRUSIONS

Magma sometimes cools below the surface. It forces its way into the sedimentary rock layers to form igneous *intrusions* (see Figure 3.9). Very large intrusions are called *batholiths*. They cool very slowly. Thinner walls of rock that cut across the 'grain' of layered rocks are called *dykes*. When magma squeezes its way between the layers, intrusions called *sills* or dome-shaped masses called *laccoliths* are formed. Over millions of years the softer sediments are eroded away by water, ice and wind.

Figure 3.9 Magma forms intrusions below ground

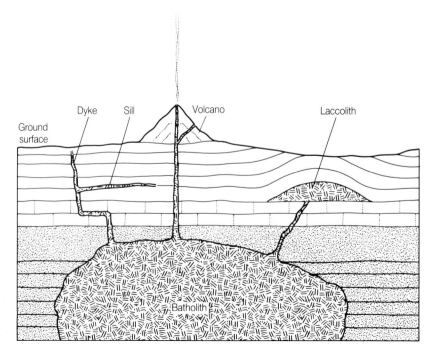

QUESTIONS ON CHAPTER 3

1 How can volcanic activity be monitored?

2 What is the difference between dykes and sills?

3 What process eventually removes the overlying layers to expose intrusions at the surface?

4 Why are most volcanoes cone shaped?

5 How does volcanic ash form?

6 What are the various ways in which volcanic ash can cause death?

7 Why do farmers find the slopes of dormant volcanoes attractive?

8 Explain how the chemistry and temperature of lava might affect both the shape and behaviour of a volcano.

9 Explain how the role of volcanoes is changing:
(a) the world's climate
(b) the composition of the atmosphere.

ROCKS AND THEIR USES

Rocks are everywhere. Not only can they be easily found on beaches, cliffs and road cuttings, but they can be seen in towns as well. These photographs (Figures 4.1–4.4) show just a few of the many varieties of rocks.

Figure 4.1 Granite

Figure 4.2 Slate

Figure 4.3 Marble

Figure 4.4 Shelly limestone

Finding local rocks

- Make a list of all the places in your area where rocks are exposed.
- Conduct a survey of your local area, looking carefully at buildings, pavements, walls, gravestones and shop fronts.
- Record examples of how rock has been used by making sketches and taking photographs.

Collecting local rocks

- Work in groups and collect some rock samples
- The best places to look for rocks are places where the earth has been disturbed or worn away by water or wind.

Do

- Wear eye protection when chipping at rocks.
- Wear a hard hat in situations where there are rocks above you.

Don't

- Collect rocks where it is unsafe to do so, e.g. under overhanging cliffs or in quarries.
- Cause damage to walls or buildings.

How to work

- Use a notebook to record where you found the rock.
- Put each sample in a labelled plastic bag, saying where it was collected and what you think it is.

Testing rock samples

- Use the samples collected in Activity 2 for investigations into the following rock properties, again working in groups. For each rock sample, record the results of each test.

Colour

- Is the sample the same colour throughout or does the colour vary?
- Is the surface colour different to the colour of a fresh surface of the rock? If so, why do you think this might be?

Texture

Some rocks look smooth, others are rough and grainy.

- Use a hand lens (x8) to look for more details – does the

rock texture give you any clues about how the rock might have formed?

Hardness

Some rocks are harder than others. You will find some rocks difficult to break and some more difficult to scratch than others.

- Use your fingernail and an iron nail to test the hardness of the samples.

Layering

- Can you see any layering? If so, what does this suggest about how the rock might have formed?

Porosity

Some rocks are porous. This means that there are many tiny holes between the rock grains that can soak up water.

- Can you think of a method you could use to compare the porosities of different rocks?

Reaction to acid

- What happens when a small amount of dilute (2 M) hydrochloric acid is dropped on to the samples? Do they all behave in the same way?

Density

You may find that some of the samples feel heavier than others. This is because they are denser. The density of a rock is its mass in grams packed into each centimetre cubed. It can be calculated as follows:

$$\text{Density (in g/cm}^3\text{)} = \frac{\text{mass (in g)}}{\text{volume (in cm}^3\text{)}}$$

- To find out the volume of the sample, place it in a measuring cylinder partly filled with water. Then see how much the water level rises on the volume scale (see Figure 4.5).

What to do next ...

- Study your results from the tests. Then try sorting the rocks into groups, based on their characteristics. It helps to label each one with a number before you start sorting.
- Discuss with your group how you think each type of rock might have been formed and what its past history might have been.

- Lay out the rock samples with written comments next to each one to show the results of your group's investigations, so that others can see them.
- Compare your presentation and results with those from other groups.

Figure 4.5 Finding the volume of a rock sample

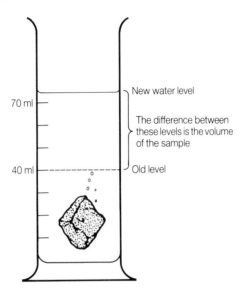

70 ml

New water level

The difference between these levels is the volume of the sample

40 ml

Old level

CLASSIFYING ROCKS

There are hundreds of different kinds of rock but scientists divide them into three main classes, according to how they formed.

Igneous rocks are made up of crystals formed by the cooling of molten magma either from volcanoes or from magma which cools below ground. These rocks are usually quite hard and the individual crystals are often visible.

Sedimentary rocks are made mainly of fragments of earlier rocks that have been worn away. They are often deposited in layers and sometimes contain fossils of earlier life forms.

Metamorphic rocks are those that have been altered by heat and pressure. They may contain crystals like igneous rocks but often have the layered appearance of sedimentary rocks.

ACTIVITY 4

Classifying your rock samples

You have already divided your rock samples up according to their similarities and differences, but how does this compare with the way scientists classify them?

- Look at the samples again and decide the rock class for each one. The key overleaf will help you to do this.

Key to classifying rock samples

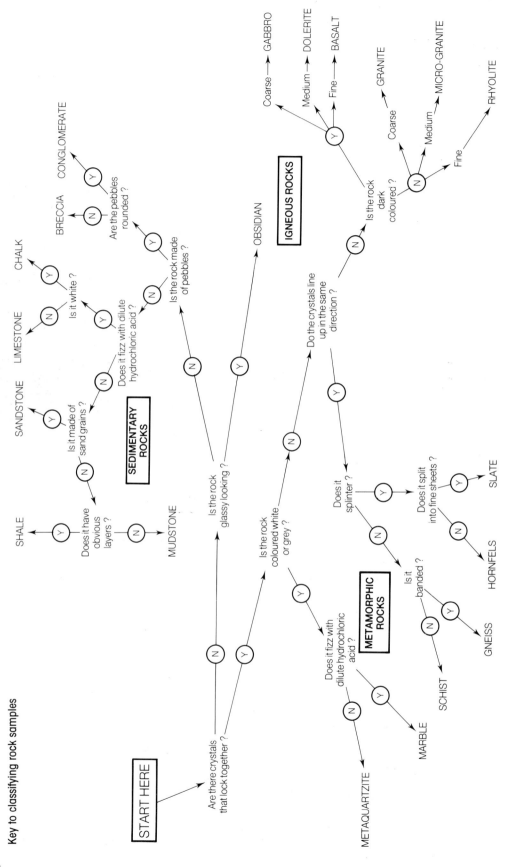

START HERE

Are there crystals that lock together ?

METAQUARTZITE

Does it fizz with dilute hydrochloric acid ?

MARBLE

Is the rock coloured white or grey ?

Is the rock glassy looking ?

OBSIDIAN

Do the crystals line up in the same direction ?

Does it splinter ?

Does it split into fine sheets ?

SLATE

HORNFELS

Is it banded ?

SCHIST

GNEISS

METAMORPHIC ROCKS

Is the rock dark coloured ?

Coarse → GABBRO

Medium → DOLERITE

Fine → BASALT

Coarse → GRANITE

Medium → MICRO-GRANITE

Fine → RHYOLITE

IGNEOUS ROCKS

Is the rock made of pebbles ?

Are the pebbles rounded ?

CONGLOMERATE

BRECCIA

Does it fizz with dilute hydrochloric acid ?

Is it white ?

CHALK

LIMESTONE

Is it made of sand grains ?

SANDSTONE

Does it have obvious layers ?

SHALE

MUDSTONE

SEDIMENTARY ROCKS

42

Looking at the uses of rocks

Rocks have many uses, either as construction materials, or as sources of raw materials for making cement and concrete (see Figure 4.6).

- Discuss the different rocks you have investigated with your group, and decide what practical uses you think they might have.

Figure 4.6 Limestone quarry – crushed limestone is used to make concrete and cement

USEFUL EARTH MATERIALS

Everything we touch and use has been made from materials that have come either directly or indirectly from the Earth. Coal and oil are often called 'fossil fuels' because they form over millions of years from the remains of animals and plants. However, these materials are not just fuels – it is possible to make perfume, aspirin, plastics and many other products from coal and oil. All the different metals we use come from the Earth's minerals. Glass comes from melted quartz sand.

Imagine how difficult our daily lives would be without plastics and metals. There would be no locks on doors, no cars, no knives and forks; no packaging around our food, no plastic bottles nor carrier bags, no electrical wiring ... the list is almost endless!

- Make lists under three headings of the objects in your home made of glass, metal and plastics.

Copper and bronze

About 6000 years ago, people discovered how to obtain and use copper. It is easier to smelt or extract than most metals because minerals containing copper only need to be heated to about 1000 °C. People probably discovered this by accident as stones containing copper oozed melted globules of metal around roaring camp fires.

ACTIVITY 6

Shaping copper

Look at some unstranded copper wire of the kind found in a 13 A cable.

- How easily does this metal bend?
- How much effort does it take to flatten the end of a piece of the wire if you hit it with a hammer on an iron block?
- What are the advantages and disadvantages of it being a soft metal?
- How successful do you think an axehead made of this metal would be for chopping down a tree?

The softness of copper was overcome by mixing it, when molten, with another very soft metal called tin. The combined metal or alloy, called bronze, was much harder than either copper or tin on its own. This was discovered about 5800 years ago in the Middle East.

Iron

The extraction of iron from iron ore requires smelting temperatures of around 1500 °C. This is probably why it was discovered later than copper or tin – about 3500 years ago. If small amounts of carbon are added to molten iron, it forms the much harder alloy called steel. Tools made of steel remained rare and little used in Europe until the eighteenth century. However, Samurai swordsmen perfected the use of steel in the twelfth century. A sword made of steel was very flexible and extremely hard. It ensured almost certain victory against an enemy with only a bronze sword. Iron is still the most widely used of all the metals, with around 800 million tonnes of iron minerals being mined each year.

Aluminium

Aluminium is found at least in small quantities in nearly every kind of rock, but it is difficult to extract. The only workable mineral is bauxite – a kind of soil very rich in aluminium oxide. Aluminium is a good conductor of electricity and is light, strong and rust-free.

- Make a list of at least ten items that are made of aluminium. You will find encyclopaedias and reference books useful.

Metal ores

A mineral ore is any useful mineral substance that is worth the time, money and effort needed to remove it from the Earth. As you will see from the next activity, a metal ore in its natural state does not always resemble the metal product.

ACTIVITY 7

Identifying four metal ores

To help you identify the four metal ores haematite, cassiterite, chalcopyrite and galena (see Figures 4.7–4.10), there are some tests that you can carry out on their properties.

Figure 4.7 Haematite
– a valuable iron ore

Figure 4.8 Cassiterite –
an ore of tin

Figure 4.9 Galena – a
silvery metal ore of lead,
with calcite (white)

Figure 4.10
Chalcopyrite – an ore
of copper

- Follow the instructions overleaf for each test and summarise your findings for each unidentified sample in a record chart (see Figure 4.11 overleaf).
- When you have found out as much as you can about the minerals, compare your findings to those shown in the table of properties on page 47 and attempt to identify the minerals.

Figure 4.11 Recording
the properties of
mineral samples

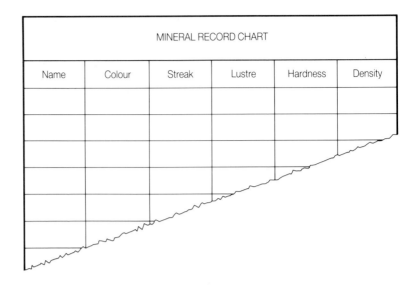

MINERAL RECORD CHART					
Name	Colour	Streak	Lustre	Hardness	Density

Colour, streak and lustre

Does each sample have the same colour throughout? What
colour is the powder of each mineral? The colour of the
powdered mineral is called the streak. The easiest way to see
the streak is to scratch the sample.

The amount of light reflected by the sample (shininess), is
called the lustre. How would you describe this property for
each mineral?

Hardness

Some minerals are harder than others. Mohs' scale (shown
below) is a list of standard minerals arranged in order of
increasing hardness. Find the hardness of the ore samples by
reference to this scale. Remember harder minerals are more
difficult to scratch.

Standard minerals	Hardness of familiar items
1 talc	
2 gypsum	fingernail 2.5
3 calcite	brass coin 3
4 fluorspar	iron nail 4
5 apatite	glass 5.5
6 feldspar	steel blade 6
7 quartz	steel file 7
8 topaz	
9 corundum	
10 diamond	

Density

Find out the density of each sample, following the method on
page 40. Most metallic minerals feel heavy and this is because

they are much denser than most other Earth materials.

- The table below summarises the main properties of four metallic ores – how does it compare with your record chart?

Mineral	Hardness	Colour	Streak	Relative density	Lustre (shininess)
Galena	2.5	Silver grey	Lead grey	7.5	Silvery
Chalcopyrite	4	Brass yellow	Greenish	4	Brassy
Haematite	5–6	Black/reddish brown	Reddish brown	5	Metallic
Cassiterite	6–7	Black/brown	Pale grey	7	Varies

EXERCISE 1

Useful metals

1) Why would people using bronze have had an advantage over people using stone tools?

2) What are the two metals that make up bronze?

3) What are the ingredients of steel?

4) How much iron ore is mined every year?

5) What is the most common iron ore?

WHERE DO MINERALS OCCUR?

Most metallic ores form as crystals during the cooling of magma or hot watery solutions. They crystallise out at different temperatures as shown in the table below.

Metal ore	Temperature of formation (°C)
Tin	350–500
Copper	300–400
Lead	200–300
Zinc	200–300
Iron	below 200

Although many minerals occur as rock-forming minerals, they are also found in mineral veins (see Figure 4.12 overleaf). Hot fluids flow through fissures (cracks) in the rocks above a heat source such as a granite intrusion. As these fluids cool, crystals of different minerals grow on the walls of the fissure. A fissure which has been filled in by crystals is called a vein.

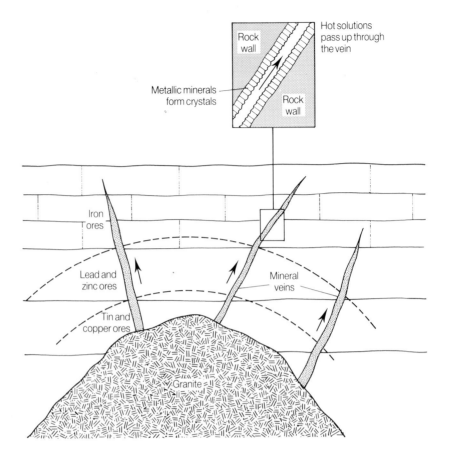

Figure 4.12 Mineral
veins above a granite
intrusion

Hot solutions
pass up through
the vein

Rock
wall

Metallic minerals
form crystals

Rock
wall

Iron
ores

Lead and
zinc ores

Mineral
veins

Tin and
copper ores

Granite

IGNEOUS ROCKS

EXERCISE 2

A closer look at igneous rocks

1) Look at a sample of granite. The different minerals have
   formed crystals of various shapes (see Figure 4.1 on
   page 38).

2) Using the descriptions below of the minerals in granite,
   make a correctly labelled sketch of the rock.

   Feldspar = light-coloured large rectangular crystals
   Quartz = glassy-looking crystals
   Biotite mica = small black speckly flaky crystals

Granite is one kind of igneous rock, but there are many other
varieties, depending on the composition of the magma, and
on the size of the crystals. Scientists think that tiny crystals
mean that a melt has cooled fast, whereas large crystals mean
that it has cooled slowly.

Figure 4.13 The texture of dolerite – note the small crystals, compared to granite

Figure 4.14 Basalt – the crystals are even smaller than those in dolerite

3) Compare the sample of granite to samples of dolerite and basalt (see Figures 4.13 and 4.14). Describe the appearance of each rock and the crystal size.

4) In each case, decide at what depth the rock might have formed.

5) Figure 4.15 (overleaf) shows an igneous rock called a porphyry. Notice the large well-formed crystals, surrounded by lots of tiny crystals. If possible, have a look at a sample of this rock.

6) From the work you have done on basalt and granite, can you explain why the porphyry has two distinct crystal sizes?

7) What do you think its cooling history might have been?

49

Figure 4.15 A porphyry

SEDIMENTARY ROCKS

The land is constantly being worn away by the movement of ice, wind, rivers and sea waves. This process loosens broken rocks which become boulders, pebbles, sand and mud. In time, this material settles as layers of sediment, to form new sedimentary rock.

ACTIVITY 8

How do sediments form?

- Mix equal amounts of sand, gravel and clay in a jar with water. Replace the cap on the jar and shake up the mixture.
- Sketch the material in the jar after it has been allowed to stand and explain why the material settles the way it does.

ACTIVITY 9

Sloppy sediment to solid rock

In time, newly deposited layers of sand or mud become hard and solid. You can find out about this by making your own 'rocks'.

- Press some damp sand into an empty yoghurt container.
- Turn this out on to a sheet of paper.
- Why does the sand stay together?
- What happens if the sand dries out?
- Repeat this procedure, mixing damp sand with small amounts of other materials such as 2 ml of salt, clay, sugar, Polyfilla or iron sulphate (see Figure 4.16). You could also try adding gravel.

Figure 4.16 Which of your 'rocks' is the hardest?

Damp sand | Damp sand + clay | Damp sand + gravel + polyfilla

- When dry, test the 'rocks' you have made to find out which is the hardest.

(Save your artificial rocks for later tests on how rocks break down in weathering – see page 60.)

Compaction

Over millions of years, the rock grains within the newly deposited layers are pushed closer together in a process called compaction, as they are squeezed by the weight of new layers above. This forces water out of the sediment and dissolved substances cement the grains together, to make the rock hard and solid. Thin layers of minerals like calcium carbonate, silica or iron oxide are left on each grain as a coating.

EXERCISE 3

A closer look at sedimentary rocks

1) Here is a list of three sedimentary rocks, but the list of materials they were formed from is in the wrong order – can you correct it?

Name of rock	Original loose material
Sandstone	gravel and pebbles
Conglomerate	mud
Shale	sand

2) Compare the 'rocks' you have made with samples of real sandstone, conglomerate, and shale, making a list of the similarities and differences.

51

Types of sedimentary rock

Organic rocks

Not all sediments come from fragments of rocks that have
been worn away. Many limestones are rocks formed from the
remains of animals and plants. Coal is also composed of
organic material, from the carbonised remains of trees and
other plants.

Chemical rocks

Sometimes deposits called evaporites may form as water
evaporates and precipitates its dissolved chemicals. This can
happen in hot dry climates in shallow seas. Lime is the first to
be deposited, followed by other salts such as gypsum and
halite (rock salt).

ACTIVITY 10

Evaporating water

What kinds of salts are left when seawater is evaporated?

- Gently heat a sample of seawater in an evaporating dish
  and do the same with samples of river and distilled water
  for comparison.
- Look at each dish and record your results.
- Halite (rock salt) and gypsum are examples of evaporite
  rocks. Make a note of their properties (colour, hardness,
  etc.).

Oolitic limestones

Most limestones are made of deposited remains of shells,
corals and other sea creatures, but some limestones have
formed directly from seawater. In tropical climates where
warm seawater evaporates, the calcium bicarbonate in the
water is deposited (precipitated) as lime (calcium carbonate)
around each sand grain. Small spheres are formed called
ooliths. Each oolith is made of a number of layers. They form
on sloping shores of tropical seas where tides roll the ooliths
up and down in the warm water. Finally they collect and are
cemented together to form oolitic limestone.

ACTIVITY 11

Studying oolitic limestone

- Look at a sample of oolitic limestone with a hand lens and
  note the size of the spheres. Compare the sample to the
  magnified photograph of oolitic limestone shown in
  Figure 4.17.

Figure 4.17 Oolitic limestone – ooliths are spheres of calcium carbonate (scale: 1 cm represents 1 mm)

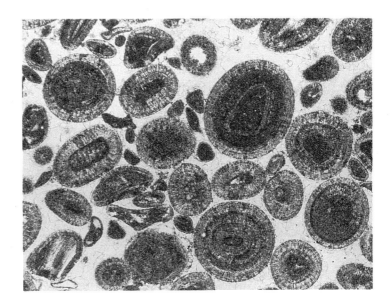

- All limestone reacts with acid. Put a drop of dilute hydrochloric acid on the sample of limestone. Do the same with some scale from a kettle. Write down what happens in each case.

METAMORPHIC ROCKS

Rocks will undergo changes in their structure and mineral grains when they are subjected to intense heat and pressure at depth. These changes produce metamorphic rocks. There is no melting in metamorphism – new crystals grow within a solid rock.

EXERCISE 4

The effect of heat

The table below shows temperature readings taken at various depths from a borehole in the Gulf (Middle East).

Depth (km)	Temperature (°C)
1	40
4	160
8	320
12	480
16	640

1) Is the temperature increasing or decreasing with depth?

2) Make a line graph of temperature against depth.

3) Predict what the temperature might be at a depth of 20 km.

4) What is the average rate of change of temperature with depth?

5) At surface pressures, rocks begin melting at 1000 °C, but high pressures often prevent this happening, so rocks can still remain solid at depths of over 40 km – what will the temperature be at this depth?

Igneous intrusions and metamorphism

Metamorphism does not just occur in deeply buried rocks. Rocks in contact with cooling magma at a volcano or next to an igneous intrusion will be baked by the heat. Figure 4.18 is a sketch map showing the zones of alteration around a granite intrusion.

Figure 4.18 Changes to rocks caused by heat from an igneous intrusion

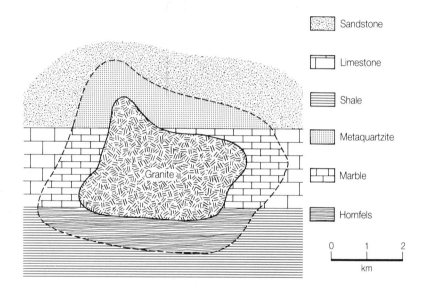

- Sandstone
- Limestone
- Shale
- Metaquartzite
- Marble
- Hornfels

0   1   2
km

Identifying changes

- Examine samples of limestone, shale, sandstone, metaquartzite, marble and hornfels using a steel point and a hand lens.
- Record the properties of each rock.
- Pair up the samples, putting one sedimentary rock and the correct metamorphic rock in each pair, and explain your decision.
- Summarise in a table what the original rocks have been altered to.
- Make a table to record the differences and similarities between the two rocks in each pair.
- Study the diagram of changes in sandstone (Figure 4.19) – describe how the sand grains have changed.

Figure 4.19
Microscopic views of
sandstone and
metaquartzite

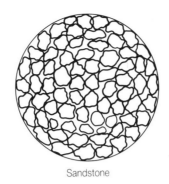 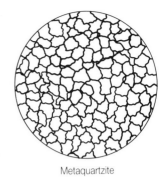

Sandstone   Metaquartzite

More about pressure

Look at samples of schist and gneiss (see Figure 4.20). Both
rocks form in conditions of very high pressure and
temperature.

Figure 4.20 Schist
(left) and gneiss
(right) – both rocks are
formed by regional
metamorphism

1) Write a description of each rock.

2) At what depth would you expect schist and gneiss to be
   formed?

3) If rocks like these form at such great depths, why is it
   possible to pick up samples of them, lying at the
   surface?

4) When there are large-scale movements of rock layers in
   fold mountain building, rocks may be carried to great
   depths over large areas and affected by both heat and
   pressure in what is known as regional metamorphism.
   Make a copy of the second sketch in Figure 4.21
   (overleaf) and shade in red the areas where there would
   be most metamorphism.

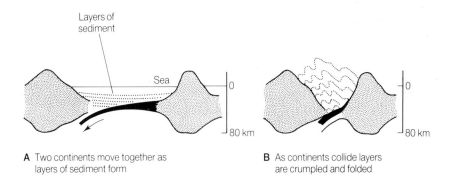

Figure 4.21 How large volumes of sedimentary rock can be affected by pressure and heat

Layers of sediment

Sea

0

80 km

0

80 km

A Two continents move together as layers of sediment form

B As continents collide layers are crumpled and folded

Uses of metamorphic rocks

Many useful materials come from metamorphic rocks and their minerals, such as diamonds and talc. People have made use of metamorphic rocks like slate and marble for hundreds of years.

● Find out more about the uses made of diamonds, talc, slate and marble. Use reference books from your local library to help you.

THE ROCK CYCLE

Rocks are continually being formed, destroyed and formed again, in an endless 'cycle' of change (see Figure 4.22). The cycle begins when molten magma reaches the surface in volcanoes, or when it pushes through rock layers to form intrusions. New igneous rocks form when the magma cools.

Figure 4.22 The rock cycle

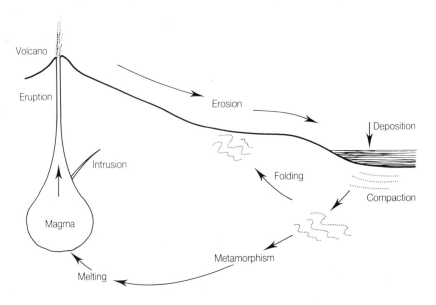

Volcano

Eruption

Erosion

Deposition

Intrusion

Folding

Compaction

Magma

Metamorphism

Melting

Wind, rain, ice and rivers slowly wear away surface rocks. Eventually previously buried intrusions become exposed, worn away and broken down into fragments such as pebbles, sand and mud. These fragments are deposited in layers, which are buried and compacted as more fragments are deposited on top. If the layers undergo sideways pressure, they will be folded. If they are buried deeply, some rocks will be changed to metamorphic rocks. Some may even melt completely to become magma. Sometimes pressures within the Earth are so great that buried rocks can be uplifted above sea-level. This has happened in the world's fold mountains – Mt Everest is made of folds of sedimentary rocks, with sea-shells, that were once on the sea-floor over 50 million years ago. It normally takes ages for a rock particle to complete one revolution of the rock cycle.

QUESTIONS ON CHAPTER 4

1 Make your own copy of Figure 4.12 on page 48 and label where you would expect the various metal ores to crystallise. Give reasons for your decisions.

2 Explain how a sloppy sediment becomes rock (see Activity 9 on p. 50 and Figure 4.22 on p. 56).

3 What are the three main origins of sedimentary rock?

4 What kind of rock is limescale from the inside of a kettle?

5 Decide if each of these statements is true or false and write out the true statements.
  Erosion is the process that wears away rocks.
  Only soft rocks are worn away.
  All erosion involves movement of rock material.

6 How many 'routes' are shown in the rock cycle diagram (Figure 4.22)?

7 Describe what would happen to one quartz pebble eroded from a granite intrusion along one 'route' you have chosen through the diagram.

8 What kinds of rock are formed by cemented and compacted sand and mud?

9 What size of crystals (coarse, medium or fine) would rocks that formed in the following situations have:
  (a) an igneous rock that cooled deep below ground;
  (b) cooled lava from a volcano.

10 Copy out Figure 4.23 and label each of the seven arrows, using these terms: cooling; erosion; compaction; folding; heat and pressure; melting; eruption and intrusion. What word is missing from the empty box?

Figure 4.23 Flow diagram of the rock cycle

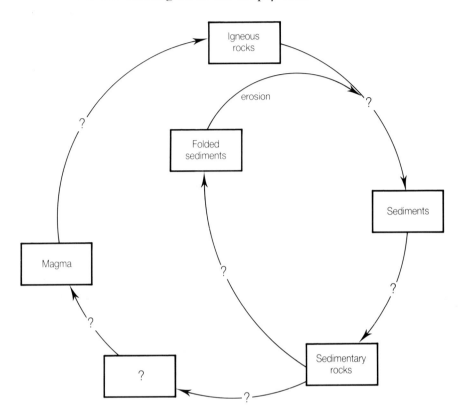

CHAPTER 5

WEATHERING AND EROSION OF ROCKS

When rocks are exposed to weather, they start to change. You can see many of these changes if you look at old buildings. Nothing stays as it is – given enough time and exposure to the weather, rocks eventually break up and crumble away.

WHAT IS WEATHERING?

Weathering is the breaking apart of rocks by physical forces and by processes of decay (rotting). The two processes are shown in the next activity.

ACTIVITY 1

Breaking up a sweet

Test out the following two ways to break up a boiled sweet.

- Wrap a sweet in paper and break it up with a hammer.
- Place the broken sweet in a beaker with warm water and stir. What eventually happens to the remains of the sweet?
- In this activity, which of the processes is 'breaking apart' and which is 'decay'? In weathering, both processes break the rock down, at the same time.

CHEMICAL WEATHERING (DECAY)

This type of weathering takes place most readily in the presence of oxygen and water. Oxygen combines with a number of minerals within rocks turning them into oxides. The same process makes iron rust.

ACTIVITY 2

How does iron rust?

- Set up three small jam jars as shown in Figure 5.1 (overleaf) and leave them for a week.
- In which jar has the nail rusted the most?
- Explain fully what you have found out.

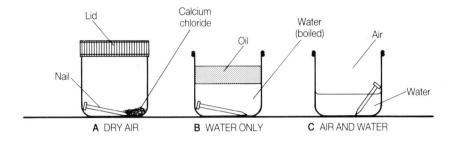

Figure 5.1 How does iron rust?

A DRY AIR   **B** WATER ONLY   **C** AIR AND WATER

In addition to oxidation, there are other ways in which rocks weather chemically. Rain-water is slightly acidic and can dissolve most rocks, given enough time.

ACTIVITY 3

How are rocks affected by water?

Even natural unpolluted rain-water is slightly acidic. You will find litmus paper or a pH meter useful for making measurements of acidity.

- Devise a test to find out what kind of water is most acidic. Later you can find out how different samples of water affect rocks.
- Collect water samples from various sources or make up test solutions in 500 ml beakers as follows:

  A = tap water
  B = alkaline water containing sodium chloride (common salt)
  C = acidic water made by adding dilute (2 M) hydrochloric acid
  D = distilled water (neutral – neither acid nor alkaline)

- Submerge various samples of limestone and sandstone in the solutions.
- Do you notice any immediate changes?
- Leave the samples overnight – how do they change? Do they dissolve or become softer and more crumbly?
- Leave the rocks which do not crumble and look at them the following day. If they still have not crumbled, remove them and allow them to dry out thoroughly. Put them back in the water for a day or so. Repeat this several times.
- Which rock is the first to crumble?
- Which rock is the most resistant?
- What kind of water affects rocks most?
- Use the solutions to test the 'rocks' you made in yoghurt pots – see Chapter 4, Activity 9 on page 50.
- Record on a bar chart how long it takes for each 'rock' to crumble.

The dissolving action of water

Limestone is one example of a rock that is affected by rain-water. It contains calcium carbonate and this reacts with the rain-water, turning it into calcium bicarbonate which is soluble. Cracks in the limestone are widened and caves are formed. The limestone cave shown in Figure 5.2 contains a mass of stalactites hanging from the roof with stalagmites on the floor of the cave. They are formed as water drips from the cave roof, re-depositing calcium carbonate as it does so.

Figure 5.2 A limestone cave with stalactites

PHYSICAL WEATHERING (BREAKING APART)

In hot deserts, alternate heating and cooling by the Sun may cause the outer layers of rocks to crumble as they first expand and then contract. This produces the loose sand and pebbles so often seen in deserts.

Frost action is another effective process for breaking rocks apart. In mountainous areas, where it is wet and cold, water freezes in cracks in the rock. It expands as it turns to ice and puts the rock on either side of a crack under great pressure – 140 kilograms per square centimetre. The crack is widened and when the ice melts, even more water can collect. This process of frost-shattering is the main kind of weathering that takes place on mountains. It is most effective at loosening stones and boulders, which fall down slopes to collect as *scree* (see Figure 5.3 overleaf).

Figure 5.3 Scree
formation

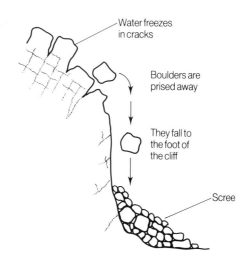

Water freezes
in cracks

Boulders are
prised away

They fall to
the foot of
the cliff

Scree

ACTIVITY 4

Frost action

- Fill a glass bottle with water and place it in a sealed thick plastic bag inside a freezer. Leave it until it is frozen.
- Then remove the bag and examine the bottle carefully.
- What has happened to the bottle? Fully explain these results.
- What have you found out about how freezing might weather rocks?

ACTIVITY 5

How much does ice expand?

- Devise a test to find out how much water increases in volume as it turns to ice, using a plastic syringe (sealed at the needle end), water and a freezer.
- How can you measure what happens? Carry out the test and record your findings.
- From your investigation, decide if ice increases in volume by about 3%, 5% or 9 %.

ACTIVITY 6

The effects of freezing and thawing

- Devise and carry out a reliable test to find out the effects of freezing and thawing on samples of shale, sandstone and granite.

Things To Think About:

A second set of samples could act as a control.
Weathering is a slow process and frost shattering works best when there is repeated freezing and thawing.

- What difference does it make if one set of samples is kept dry?
- Record your method and findings.

How long does weathering take?

- Survey the gravestones in your local churchyard or cemetery. The readability of the dates will give you a clue about the rate of weathering. Use a grading system like this (see Figure 5.4):

A = perfect lettering;
B = edges of lettering damaged;
C = hard to read, some letters missing;
D = unreadable.

Figure 5.4 Weathering in the graveyard

- Use a chart like this to record your findings:

Rock-type	Date	Amount of weathering
e.g. limestone	1899	C

- Show your results on a scatter-graph – explain the pattern you see.
- Did you find that certain rock-types weather faster than others?
- Produce separate scatter-graphs for different gravestone rock-types.
- Explain your findings.

WHAT HAPPENS TO THE BROKEN WEATHERED ROCK PIECES?

Weathered rocks are usually softer and more broken than 'fresh' unweathered rocks, so they are worn down much more quickly by water, ice, wind and wave action. This process is called *erosion*.

EXERCISE 1

Examples of erosion

1) Make a list of the everyday examples of erosion mentioned in this short story – how many can you spot?

   'Mum sent me to the butchers on my bike. I skidded going round a bend. I'm going to have to buy a new tyre soon – the tread on it is almost gone. I don't know why the butcher doesn't throw his knife away. He has sharpened it so often that the blade is really thin. He chops the joints on a wooden bench that has a big hollow in the middle of it. The stone steps are a short cut back to my house. That's odd! They are also hollowed in the middle where people have walked. My shoes leak – I must get new soles. Mum won't be pleased!'

2) Try to think of some other examples of your own.

How erosion happens

At the same time as rocks are being softened by weathering, they are being worn away by moving water, ice and wind, and deep valleys may be carved out. These changes usually take place over thousands of years.

Where the material comes to rest

Most erosion takes place where rocks are most exposed, i.e. on high mountains. Ice sheets and rivers erode rocks as they flow downhill to the sea, carrying pebbles, sand and mud in huge quantities. Most of the eroded material comes to rest either on lowland areas or on the sea floor, as layers of sediment.

STREAMS AND RIVERS

Water is very effective at washing away loose rock material. As boulders, pebbles and sand are washed downhill by the current, they may cause even more erosion – river beds are deepened and widened (see Figure 5.5).

Figure 5.5 A river
erodes it's channel –
circular pothole
(18 cm in diameter) in
river bed, photo-
graphed in dry season

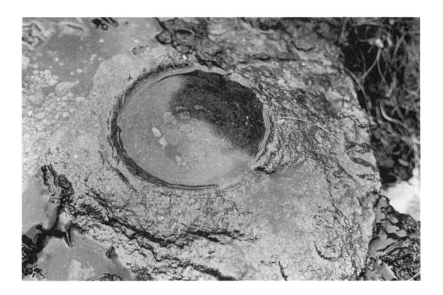

The flow of water under gravity not only gives rivers the power to cut steep-sided valleys, it also makes them very good at moving material. This material is called the river's load. It consists of boulders, pebbles, sand, mud and dissolved material. As the pebbles bounce along in the current, they hit the bed and banks of the river. Swirling river currents may pick up pebbles and spin them around in whirlpools, to form circular holes in the river bed called potholes (see Figure 5.6). In time, the potholes widen and join together, to lower the river bed.

Figure 5.6 Pothole formation

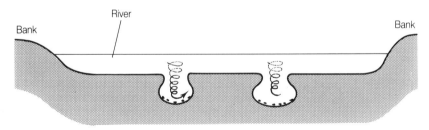

A Cracks are widened into circular potholes by swirling pebbles

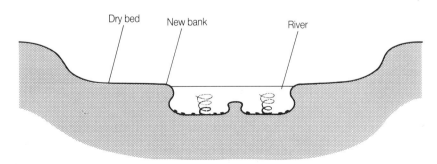

B Neighbouring potholes are eroded until they join up, and the whole river bed is lowered

Deposition

The River Mississippi carries 1000 million cubic metres of sediment into the sea every year – eroded from every part of its huge drainage basin. As the river enters the sea, the current slows and the sediment is dumped to form a delta. Deltas are found at the mouths of many rivers, if there are no strong ocean currents. When sediment is dumped in slow-moving water, it often causes the river to split into many smaller channels called distributaries.

ACTIVITY 8

How does the load settle?

- Taking care and using a plastic bottle, collect some cloudy river water from your local stream when it is in flood.
- Allow the load to settle in a measuring cylinder.
- Record and explain the pattern the particles make as they settle.
- How long does the finer silt take to settle?
- When the water looks clear, evaporate 5 ml of it on a watch glass. What do you see? What part of the river's load is this?

ACTIVITY 9

How does a river erode?

- Set up a plastic or wooden stream tray, at least 20 cm by 30 cm and about 8 cm deep (see Figure 5.7).

Figure 5.7 How does running water erode?

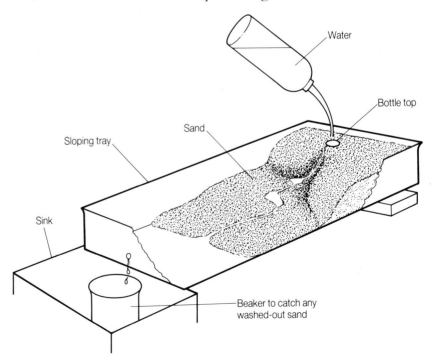

Water

Bottle top

Sand

Sloping tray

Sink

Beaker to catch any washed-out sand

- Position the sloping tray with the outlet hole over a sink, and fill the top end of the tray with damp sand.
- Trickle water on to the bottle top.
- Record how the 'river' erodes and transports the sand.
- Sketch and describe your results.
- What happens if you make the slope steeper, or mix gravel with the sand?

EXERCISE 2

Waterfalls

Waterfalls are often caused by hard bands of rock crossing the river bed. Figure 5.8 shows what happens at the Lumb Falls near Hebden Bridge in West Yorkshire.

1) Make a copy of Figure 5.8, labelling the hard band of sandstone and the softer shales.

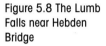

Figure 5.8 The Lumb Falls near Hebden Bridge

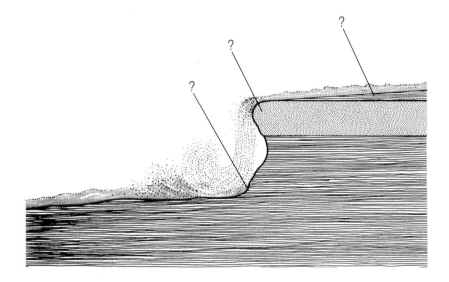

2) In which direction does the river flow? Show this with an arrow on your sketch.

3) Sketch how this area might have looked before the river began to erode.

ACTIVITY 10

Why do waterfalls form?

- Use a stream tray to make a model of a waterfall, using a layer of clay at least 1 mm thick to represent the hard band of rock.
- What happens where the clay layer is, when you add the water?
- Sketch the model and label the river valley, the waterfall and the hard and soft rocks.

AVALANCHES AND LANDSLIDES

Transport of weathered rocks under gravity is at its most dramatic in avalanches and landslides that send snow, rocks and boulders hurtling down mountain slopes. The cause of an avalanche may be a thaw, or simply the weight of snow. The worst landslide ever was started by an earthquake in Kansu province, China in 1920. It killed 180 000 people. In 1970, an avalanche in Peru buried the town of Yungay under 10 m of mud, killing 18 000 people (see Figure 5.9).

Figure 5.9 The Yungay disaster

ICE SHEETS AND GLACIERS

Ice covers one tenth of the world's land area. Most of this consists of the polar ice-caps, but snow in mountainous areas piles up and is pressed down by the weight of more snow. The lower layers turn into ice and start to slowly slide down the mountainside. A slowly moving 'river' of ice is called a glacier. Glaciers have sharp rock fragments embedded on their undersides and slowly scrape over the land like huge sheets of sand-paper. In doing so, huge amounts of rock can be removed. As glaciers move downhill, they cut deep straight U-shaped valleys (see Figure 5.10).

Rock debris, called moraine, falls on top of a glacier and gets carried along. At the end of a glacier, this material is dropped as the ice melts. Much of the deposit is boulder-clay – a mixture of clay, rocks and finely ground down material. Meltwater streams may grade and sort some of the moraine according to grain size (see Figure 5.11).

- Gravel beds are common near to the melting ice but silt is carried further away – why is this?

Figure 5.10 Ice has the power to cut out deep valleys

Figure 5.11 Features formed by melting ice

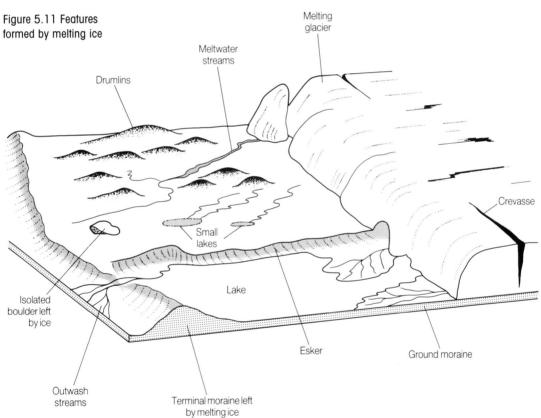

Melting glacier

Meltwater streams

Drumlins

Crevasse

Small lakes

Isolated boulder left by ice

Lake

Outwash streams

Esker

Ground moraine

Terminal moraine left by melting ice

The Ice Age

Ten thousand years ago the world was a much colder place and much of Britain and northern Europe was covered by ice sheets. The British landscape underwent considerable change, as former river valleys were deepened, widened and straightened by glaciers. The scenery of the Lake District is the result of glacial erosion, with lakes filling the troughs and valleys cut by ice.

WIND

In deserts or on sandy beaches, wind blows dust and sand against bare rocks. This sand-blasting action can wear away the softer layers, especially near the ground. Sand dunes form when the sand piles up and they migrate across the land surface. Strong winds can even blow beach sand inland to form dunes along British coasts.

WAVES AND CURRENTS

Waves will pick up sand and pebbles, hurling the material against cliffs with great force and so breaking off more rock fragments. Once material from the cliff has been eroded, sea currents and tidal movements transport loose fragments great distances.

QUESTIONS ON CHAPTER 5

1   What are the two main processes involved in weathering?

2   Are caves in limestone caused by chemical or physical weathering?

3   Only small amounts of dissolved limestone are redeposited in caves. What happens to the rest of the material that is dissolved away?

4   What are the three main agents or forces of erosion?

5   Explain, with notes and a diagram, how waterfalls are formed.

6   Each of the sentences below contains a deliberate mistake. Rewrite them, replacing the errors with the correct words.

Loose rocks at the foot of a slope are called dunes.
A pothole is cut by pebbles caught up in a whirlwind.
The Lumb Falls are caused by a hard band of limestone.
Rivers erode U-shaped valleys.
Ice covers 20% of the world's land surface.
Glaciers carve out deep V-shaped valleys.

7   Use a camera or a sketch-pad to record the landforms near your home or school. In each case, decide what kind of process has been involved in its formation.

CHAPTER

6

WATER ON THE LAND

The water cycle is the circulation of water as it changes from a liquid to water vapour and back again (see Figure 6.1). The process begins when the Sun's heat evaporates moisture. As water vapour rises it cools and condenses, to form tiny water droplets in the clouds. Rain and snow return moisture to the oceans. Strangely the environment with the least of the world's water is the atmosphere. Only 0.001% of the Earth's atmosphere is water vapour, yet this is enough to affect weather patterns, giving cloud and rain over much of the world.

Figure 6.1 The water cycle

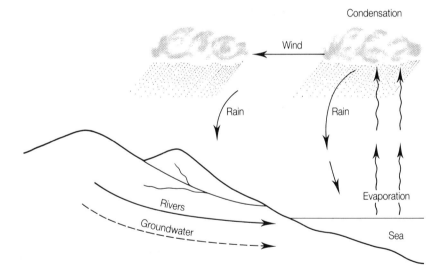

The world's water

1) Show the figures listed below on a bar chart or a pie chart.
   Oceans 97.0%
   Ice-sheets 2.0%
   Groundwater 0.5%
   Lakes and rivers 0.5%

2) Where is most of the world's water?

3) Figure 6.2 shows the water cycle in more detail. Study it carefully, then rewrite the following statements, correcting any mistakes.
    (a) 84% of all water vapour evaporates from the land and 16% evaporates from the sea.
    (b) Most of the moisture that evaporates is carried by winds to the land, where it falls as rain.
    (c) Rivers carry 77% of the water back to the sea.

Figure 6.2 Exchanges in the water cycle system (the figures show the percentage of water involved)

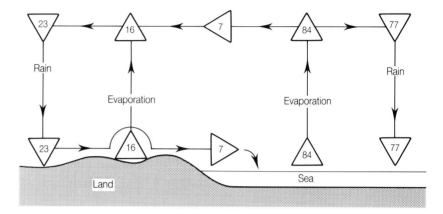

4) From the information shown in Figures 6.1 and 6.2, is most evaporation taking place over the land or over the oceans? Give your reasons.

5) Draw two pie charts:
    (a) to show the proportion of evaporation over land and sea;
    (b) to show the difference in rainfall over land and sea.

6) Make a copy of Figure 6.1 and label it to show the fastest and slowest routes through the cycle.

7) Estimate the time involved along each route, giving reasons. How does this compare with the time involved in the rock cycle?

WHERE DOES THE RAIN FALL?

Although rainfall returns most moisture directly to the oceans, the land still receives around 40 000 km³ of rain every year. This does not fall equally over the land. Coastlines are often the wettest places, as moist winds are blowing off the sea. Inland continental areas have far less rain. This explains why 32% of the land surface is desert and therefore too dry for growing crops. Another 17% of the land surface is either frozen or under ice.

• Show these figures on a bar or a pie chart.

Land moisture

Three-quarters of all the water that falls as rain or snow on the land is stored as ice in glaciers and polar ice-caps. This water is released when the ice melts. Rocks and the soil hold 24.5% as groundwater.

1) Use the information above to calculate the percentage of fresh water held in lakes and rivers.

2) Make a pie chart entitled 'What happens to rainfall on land'.

HOW DOES RAIN BECOME GROUNDWATER?

Soils or rocks which allow water to pass through them easily are said to be *permeable*. Finer grained rocks and soils have fewer air spaces and therefore tend to be *impermeable*. When rain-water soaks through the soil into the rocks beneath, it becomes *groundwater*.

Measuring permeability

A typical soil is a mixture of broken-down rock and humus – the decayed remains of plants. Water soaks into the air spaces between the soil grains. The rate at which it does so depends on:
(a) the size of the soil particles;
(b) how moist the soil is in the first place.

- Study Figure 6.3 – which soil is likely to be the more permeable of the two? Explain your answer.

Figure 6.3 Magnified view of two types of soil

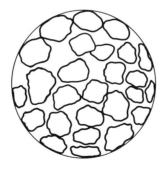
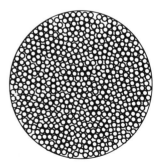

Soil permeability rates

Collect samples of three soils with different textures, such as a fine-grained clayey soil, a coarser-grained sandy soil and a *loam* (this is a soil with a mixture of both coarse and fine grains).

- Set up the samples as shown in Figure 6.4, then allow 500 ml of water to filter through each sample.

Figure 6.4 Which type of soil has the highest permeability rate?

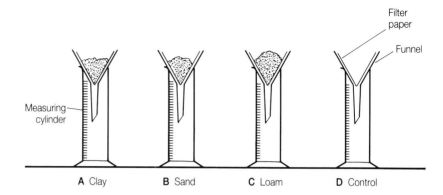

Filter paper

Funnel

Measuring cylinder

A Clay   **B** Sand   **C** Loam   **D** Control

- Record the time it takes for this amount of water to filter through each sample. From this you can work out a *permeability rate* for each soil in millilitres per second.
- Make bar charts of your results and explain your findings.
- Test out various brands of gardening compost to find out which is the most permeable, using this procedure.

Things to think about:
Should each soil sample be moist or dry at the start?
What is the reason for cylinder D?

Soil permeability outside

Soil in the laboratory has obviously been disturbed – a more accurate way to test for permeability is in the field.

- First you need a large catering tin can, with the top and bottom removed by a tin opener so that it is a cylinder. Take care to avoid sharp edges.
- Place a length of wood across the top of the can and push it into the soil to a depth of at least 6 cm.
- Place a millimetre ruler vertically in the can.
- Pour a litre of water into the can, then use a stopwatch to measure how long it takes for the water to soak in.
- Write down the depth of water in the can at intervals, e.g. every 15 seconds. From this you can work out a permeability rate in millimetres per second.
- When all the water has soaked in, repeat the procedure. Does the second litre soak away faster or more slowly?
- What is the soak-in rate in millimetres per minute?

- Draw a line graph to show the changes in the permeability rate.
- Use this technique to carry out your own fieldwork – for example, you might investigate which part of the school grounds has the most permeable soil, or whether rain-water takes longer to soak in if the soil is already moist from wet weather.

EXERCISE 3

Comparing permeability rates

1) Study Figure 6.5 – which line graph represents a sandy soil and which represents a clayey soil? Give your reasons.

2) Explain the pattern of the line graphs.

3) Copy Figure 6.5 and sketch in the line graph you would expect for a loam.

Figure 6.5
Permeability rates in two types of soil

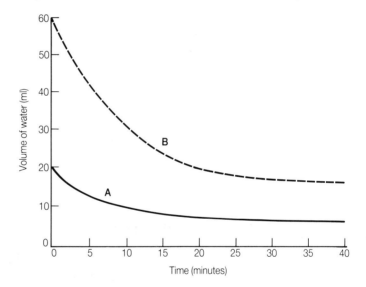

WATER IN THE ROCKS

Some water will eventually soak into the rocks and become groundwater. Rocks like sandstone and limestone are usually permeable, and water passes through them easily. In sandstone, there are air spaces between the grains and the water seeps into these pores. Sandstone is one example of a porous rock. Other rocks such as limestone and granite are not porous, but they are still permeable because water can flow through joints and cracks instead. Fine-grained rocks like shale or mudstone have rock particles packed so closely that water can hardly flow through them at all – in other words they are impermeable.

The porosity of rocks

- Find out how the porosity of different rocks varies by dropping samples of sandstone, shale, granite and limestone into water in a measuring cylinder.
- Leave each sample submerged for several hours, then remove them from the water, being careful to avoid loss of water from the cylinder.
- Why might it be important to begin this investigation with samples that are completely dry?
- How could you measure the volume of water each sample soaks up?
- What immediate clues are there to tell you if a sample is porous?
- If the rock is porous, will the reading to be higher or lower than at the start? Give your reasons.
- Using your data, calculate a porosity value for each rock sample as follows:

$$\text{Porosity (\%)} = \frac{\text{volume of water absorbed} \times 100}{\text{volume of rock}}$$

To do this you need to know the volume of the rock – use the method described on page 40 to find the volume of each sample.

- Produce a table to show the samples you have tested in order of their porosities, from highest to lowest.
- Make a full report on your findings.

AQUIFERS

Underground layers of permeable rock which are able to soak up and store water easily are called aquifers. Water soaks downwards from the surface until it reaches an impermeable rock layer. When every space within a permeable rock is filled with water, it is said to be saturated. The top of the saturated zone is called the water table (see Figure 6.6). The height of the water table varies.

- When will the water table be highest – in very wet or dry weather?

The water table usually follows the shape of the ground, curving upwards under hills and flattening out under plains.

Where the water table reaches the surface, water flows out into springs, lakes or rivers.

Figure 6.6 The water table marks the level of saturation in a permeable rock

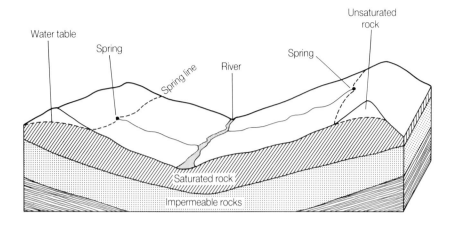

ARTESIAN WELLS AND BASINS

A downward-folding aquifer cannot lose water to impermeable layers above or below it and it forms a structure called an artesian basin (see Figure 6.7). Rain falls on the hills and soaks downwards creating a 'head' of pressure. If a well is drilled, the water gushes out in a fountain. In time the pressure lessens as more water is removed. Eventually the water has to be pumped out.

Figure 6.7 An artesian basin

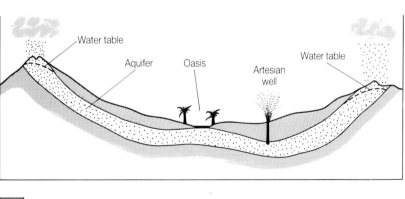

If the aquifer reaches the surface naturally, it will form an oasis. Artesian aquifers are an important source of water in dry hot deserts, e.g. the Sahara and inland Australia.

RIVERS

Rivers complete the water cycle by carrying water back to the sea from the land. The source of many rivers is a spring where groundwater from rocks reaches the surface again (see Figure 6.8). In some cases the source is a melting glacier.

Figure 6.8 The Chalk/Gault Clay junction in southern England

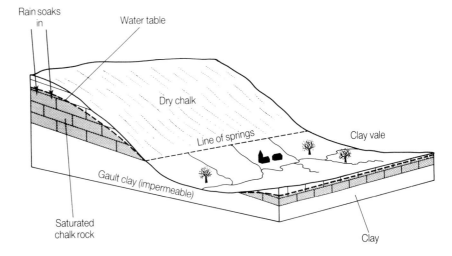

How a river system works

The area drained by a river and its tributaries is known as a drainage basin (see Figure 6.9). Some of the rain falling

Figure 6.9 The drainage basin of the River Hindburn in north Lancashire

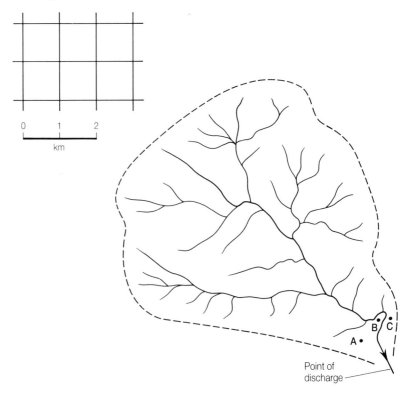

78

within the area of the drainage basin will soak into the rocks to become groundwater and some will evaporate. The rest of the water runs off into one of the channels. The drainage basin is a system where the input is the water received by rainfall and the main output is the river water flowing from the basin to the sea. When a large volume of water is discharged from a river basin in a period of heavy rain, the main river may overflow its banks and cause flooding.

Measuring inputs and outputs

Just 1 mm of rainfall in the area of a drainage basin will produce a huge volume of water at the discharge point. Volume is measured in cubic metres (m³). If each square kilometre (km²) in a drainage basin receives 1 mm of rain, then the volume of water can be calculated as follows:

$$\text{Volume of water (m}^3) = \text{area x rainfall}$$
$$= 1 \text{ km}^2 \times 1 \text{ mm}$$
$$= 1000 \text{ m} \times 1000 \text{ m} \times 0.001 \text{ m}$$
$$= 1000 \text{ m}^3$$

1) Copy the area grid shown in Figure 6.9 on to tracing paper and extend it by moving the tracing paper and then copying more squares. Then overlay the grid on the map of the drainage basin.

2) Count up the squares to find out the total area of the drainage basin.

3) Use the formula above to calculate the input for the drainage basin with a rainfall of:
   (a) 1 mm;
   (b) 5 mm.

4) The amount of rainfall which would cause the river to flood is not always the same. Decide in which of the following examples the river would flood:
   (a) a rainfall of 5 mm in one hour – in the previous five days there has been steady and prolonged rainfall;
   (b) a rainfall of 5 mm in one hour – the previous five days have been dry.

   Explain your answer.

5) Planners have decided to build a small town within the drainage basin and you are asked to advise them on the best site, making your selection from A, B and C in Figure 6.9. Produce a report with a map, marking your recommended site. Give reasons for your decisions.

Measuring rain input

- Choose a stream on a local map and work out the area of its drainage basin. For later fieldwork, if possible choose a stream which is shallow enough to cross.
- Carry out measurements of rainfall in your chosen drainage basin using a rain gauge (see Figure 6.10). This can be home made, using a funnel, a large can and a smaller container to collect the water. To calculate the volume of rain collected, measure in centimetres the diameter of the funnel (D), the diameter of the water container (d) and the height of the water in the container (h), and use the formula:

$$\text{Rainfall (cm}^3) = \frac{d^2 \times h}{D^2}$$

Once you have worked out d^2/D^2 all you need to do is multiply this by the height of the water collected each time.
- If possible, measure the rainfall over several days and keep careful records.
- Use this data to calculate the drainage basin rain input each day.

Figure 6.10 A rain gauge

Measuring stream output

- Place markers at each end of a 10 m length of the bank of the stream.
- Use a stopwatch to time an orange floating down in the current between the two markers.
- How many metres does the orange travel in one second? This gives you the speed of the current (C) in metres per second.

- Stretch a tape measure across the stream and measure the depth every half metre as you cross (see Figure 6.11).
- From these measurements, draw out the cross-sectional area of the stream on graph paper.
- Count up the squares to find the cross-sectional area (*A*) in square metres.
- The discharge of the stream in cubic metres per second = $A \times C$

EXERCISE 5

Calculating discharge

- How wide is the stream shown in Figure 6.11?
- What is the discharge of this stream if the flow rate is 0.5 m/s and the cross sectional area is 20 m²?

Figure 6.11 Measuring the water current, stream width, depth and cross-sectional area

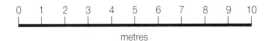

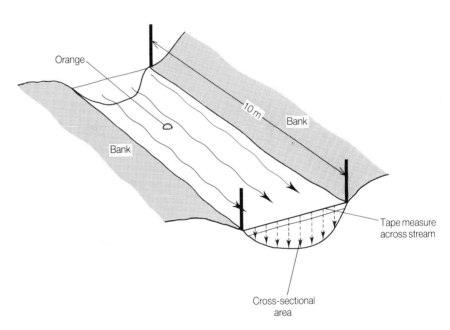

QUESTIONS ON CHAPTER 6

1 Make a copy of Figure 6.12 (overleaf) and complete the diagram using these words:

evaporation   wind   rain   run-off   cloud   sea

2 (a) Figure 6.12 (overleaf) does not show groundwater flow – adapt your copy to show this extra information.

(b) Also adapt your diagram to show the route for evaporation from the land.

Figure 6.12 Flow diagram of the water cycle

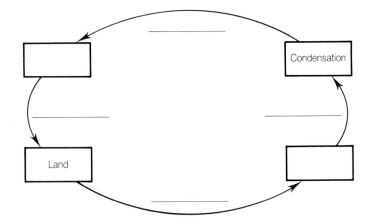

3 Arrange this list of soils in order of their permeability:
a dry clay soil after a summer drought;
a sandy loam after a period of heavy rain;
a clayey soil after a period of heavy rain;
a dry sandy soil.
Explain your reasons.

4 Figure 6.13 shows the rate at which water soaked into the soil during a storm:

Figure 6.13 Rainfall and the permeability rate

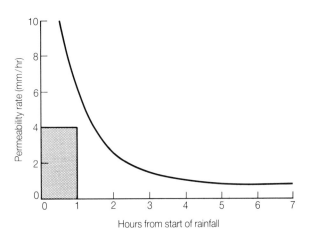

Hours from start of rainfall

(a) Explain fully the shape of the line graph.
(b) Rainfall for the first hour is shown in bar graph form – copy the diagram and complete a bar graph for each hour using the figures in the following table.

Hour	1	2	3	4	5	6
Rainfall	4	2	7	5	7	3

(c)   What is the total amount of rainfall which did not soak into the ground?

(d)   What would happen to this extra water?

5   How does water pass through non-porous rocks like limestone?

6   Explain why water gushes out of an artesian well under pressure.

7   Explain how a drainage basin system works, including inputs and outputs in your explanation.

8   Write to your local water company asking for information on sources of local water supply.

CHAPTER 7

EARTHQUAKES

An earthquake is sudden violent shaking of the ground caused by movements of underground rocks. You will see why earthquakes are such a hazard in the following account of an earthquake in San Francisco.

SAN FRANCISCO – A CITY AT RISK

Ever since the great earthquake of 1906 when most of the city was destroyed and 700 people killed, San Francisco has lived on a knife edge. In those days the city was a small town – today it is a large city. Everyone knew that one day the earth would move again with the chance that thousands would die. On 17 October 1989 it finally happened. A powerful earthquake struck Santa Cruz just south of San Francisco, killing 280 people and injuring over 600. The main quake lasted only 15 seconds but this was long enough for the top tier of the highway Interstate 880 to collapse and crush cars and people on the road below (see Figure 7.1).

Figure 7.1 The roof's fallen in – collapse of the two-tier road, San Francisco

This is how one newspaper reported the tragedy:

THE DAY THAT TIME RAN OUT

More than 250 people died when a mile of the two-tier highway collapsed at Oakland, near San Francisco. Many drivers were crushed in a concrete sandwich. The earthquake struck at 5.04 p.m. during the rush hour. Rescuers clawed with their bare hands to drag victims from the rubble.

Police patrolman Rick Andreoeti said: "It's not a matter of pulling people out but prising them out."

Leroy Fitzgerald, who works nearby, said, "You could hear it crunching down, and you could hear people screaming – but you couldn't see anything. It was just a big white cloud."

Don Sharp was driving on the bridge when his car started to shudder. "I looked in my rear view mirror and cars just vanished – plunging into the water as I looked."

What caused the disaster?

The Santa Cruz earthquake happened because of a sudden movement along a fault called the San Andreas Fault (see Figure 7.2). This fault is the boundary between two huge sections of the Earth's crust, known as plates. These are moving in opposite directions at a rate of 5.5 cm/year. The Pacific Plate is moving north as the American Plate is moving south. This is a jerky movement and each jerk produces an

Figure 7.2 The San Andreas Fault

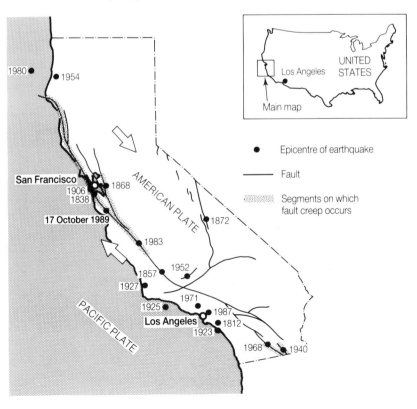

earthquake. Between earthquakes, the stress builds up in the rocks on each side of the fault, and there could be several years with no movement at all. One 200 km section of the fault has not moved since 1857 – when it finally 'breaks' a tremendous amount of stored energy will be suddenly released.

- How many years have gone by with no movement?
- Calculate the total possible movement along this section if the 'break' occurred in 1995. (Solution on p. 93.)

THE EARTHQUAKE THREAT

Figure 7.3 shows where most of the world's earthquakes have occurred. As with volcanoes (see Figure 3.8), you will see that most earthquakes occur along narrow linear belts, so there are many places where earthquakes are relatively rare. There may be 20 000 earthquakes each year but most of these are tiny tremors. Only about 20 per year are really severe. These severe earthquakes mostly occur in mountainous regions where they affect few people. On average there is only one disastrous earthquake each year in more densely populated areas, but in the last 40 years earthquakes have killed over 60 000 people, usually by the collapse of houses.

Figure 7.3 The world's earthquakes – each dot represents the epicentre of an earthquake

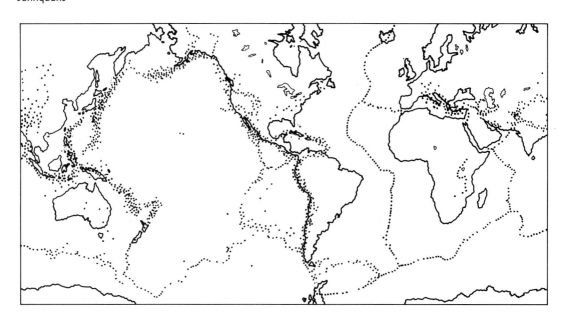

There are more deaths than ever before, not because the number of earthquakes has increased, but rather because cities in earthquake-prone areas have become more crowded.

Some of the world's worst earthquakes this century are listed in the following table.

Date	Event	Deaths
18 April 1906	San Francisco, USA	700
28 July 1976	Tangshan, China	250 000
4 March 1977	Bucharest, Romania	1541
23 November 1980	Southern Italy	2735
19/20 Sept. 1985	Twin quakes, Mexico City	8000
7 December 1988	Armenia, USSR	25 000

Probably the worst earthquake ever was in Shaanxi, China in 1556 when 830 000 people were killed.

HOW ARE EARTHQUAKES MEASURED?

One way to measure earthquakes is to record the amount of damage they do. The damage can be compared with an *intensity* scale first devised by Mercalli in 1902. Lines of equal destruction can be drawn around the centre of an observed earthquake to map out where the damage has been the most severe. These are known as *isoseismal lines* (see Figure 7.4). The *focus* is the underground source of an earthquake and the *epicentre* is the nearest point at the surface to that source.

Figure 7.4 Isoseismal lines (the numerals refer to the Mercalli scale)

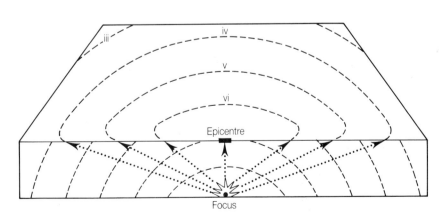

The Richter scale measures the total energy release of an earthquake – known as the magnitude – rather than the damage it does. Each whole number rise on the scale stands for a ten-fold increase in the size of the earthquake shock waves produced. The table below shows roughly how the two scales compare.

Mercalli	Description	Richter
i	only detected by seismographs	2
ii	felt by sensitive people	3.5
iii	vibrations like a passing lorry	
iv	loose objects shake	4
v	strong enough to ring church bells	
vi	some windows broken; frightening	5
vii	walls and plaster crack	
viii	chimneys fall; difficult to stand	6
ix	ground cracks; pipes burst	
x	most buildings damaged; roads crack	7
xi	disastrous: buildings destroyed, roads, railways, pipes and cables destroyed; water dams damaged	
xii	total destruction; ground rises and falls in waves	8+

Seismometers

Instruments called *seismometers* record the total energy released in an earthquake, as measured on the Richter scale. The Santa Cruz earthquake registered 6.9 on this scale. Seismometers can detect even faint vibrations. One early type was the rod seismometer (see Figure 7.5). It was made up of a number of cylindrical columns of differing heights and thicknesses.

Figure 7.5 Two types of seismometer

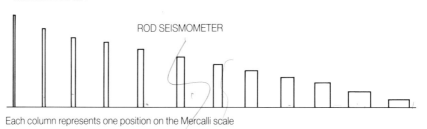

ROD SEISMOMETER

Each column represents one position on the Mercalli scale

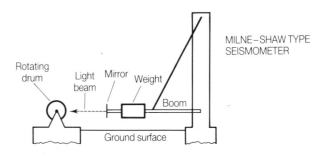

MILNE–SHAW TYPE SEISMOMETER

Making a seismometer

- Make your own rod seismometer using wooden dowel rods of varying lengths and diameters. Stand them upright on a desk top.
- Pretend there is an earthquake by banging the desk top with your fist.
- How many rods fall in:
  (a) a slight 'earthquake'
  (b) a severe 'earthquake'?

In later seismometer designs (see Figure 7.5), a continuous recording was made as a line graph on a rotating drum, so the time and duration of the earthquake was known. One problem with this design was that all parts of the instrument vibrated in an earthquake, giving distorted readings. Modern seismometers are electronic instruments designed to avoid this problem. Vibrations are fed as electrical signals to a computer and a graphical read-out known as a seismogram is produced (see Figure 7.6).

Figure 7.6 A seismogram of an earthquake

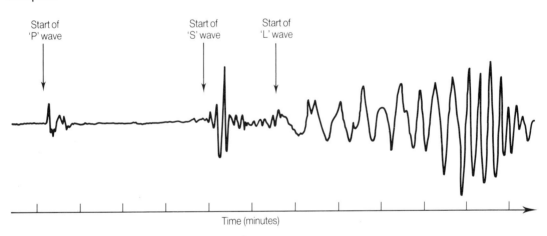

Note the three distinct pulses of shock shown in the diagram. These are caused by three different kinds of seismic wave known as P, S and L waves. They all travel in different ways.

- Which of the three types of wave travels the fastest? Which travels the slowest? How can you tell?

Typical speeds are 8 km per second for P waves, and 4 km per second for S waves. P waves can travel through solids and liquids but S waves can only travel through solid rock.

L (long) waves are confined to the surface rocks. They are the slowest of all, and do the most damage because the solid ground is sent into rolling waves. Huge cracks open at the surface only to close a few seconds later.

USING SEISMIC WAVES TO 'SEE' THE EARTH'S STRUCTURE

It is possible to study the behaviour of P and S waves as they travel through the Earth and find out what the Earth is like inside (see Figure 7.7). This is how we know there is an outer crust, with the mantle beneath and finally the core at the Earth's centre. As P and S waves travel deeper, they speed up as they pass through denser rocks. At the point where P and S waves reach the core, S waves disappear completely. It is likely that the outer core is liquid because S waves are unable to travel through it. When P waves reach the outer core, they are bent inwards because they are forced to travel through much denser rocks. This creates a 'shadow zone' at the surface where P and S waves are not recorded. The same bending effect can be seen when light rays pass from less dense air to denser water. The inner core was discovered when very faint P waves that had bounced off the inner core were recorded inside the shadow zone.

Figure 7.7 How P and S waves travel through the Earth

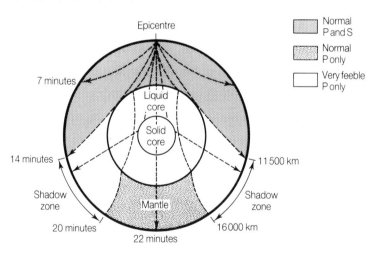

The surface distance from epicentre to shadow zone is shown. The time taken for P waves to arrive back at the surface is shown in minutes.

EXERCISE 1

Clues to the Earth's structure

1) What clues reveal that the outer core is a liquid?

2) Why do the speeds of P and S waves increase with depth?

Creating a 'shadow zone'

Make a model of what happens to shock waves as they pass into the mantle by shining a torch through a beaker of water.

- How does the beaker focus the light?
- What is the cause of the 'shadow zone'?
- What kind of shock waves do the light rays represent?
- How does the pattern you see compare with the Earth's shadow zone, as shown in Figure 7.7?

EFFECTS OF EARTHQUAKES

Tsunamis

When there is an earthquake below the sea bed, the seismic waves will cause a sudden movement of sea water. This produces a giant sea wave known as a *tsunami*. In the 1964 Alaskan earthquake, giant sea waves over 10 m high hit the coast and boats were carried several kilometres inland. The map in Figure 7.8 shows how tsunami wave fronts crossed the Pacific Ocean. Tsunamis are a great threat to human life – especially in coastal areas. There is an early warning station at Hawaii that warns countries at risk of approaching tsunamis. The whole depth of the ocean is involved in the wave motion (see Figure 7.9), but tsunamis are only really

Figure 7.8 Tsunami wave fronts cross the Pacific Ocean, a distance of 15 000 km. (Time is shown in hours)

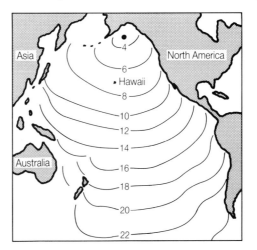

Figure 7.9 The wave height changes at a shallowing coastline

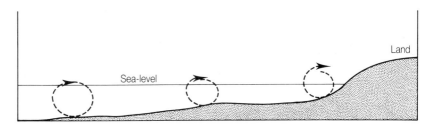

91

dangerous in shallowing water – can you see why? Wave heights of up to 30 m have been recorded.

Avalanches

Earthquakes often occur in mountainous areas where they easily dislodge loose rocks and snow. In the 1970 Peruvian earthquake, the people of Yungay were actually able to see an avalanche start in the mountains above the town, triggered by an earthquake. Sadly, not many of them managed to escape in time and the avalanche tore through the town, burying everything in a mixture of mud, ice and rocks (see Figure 5.9 on page 68).

LIVING WITH EARTHQUAKES

The collapse of the two-tier highway near San Francisco (described at the start of this chapter) could have been prevented if the support structures had been stronger.

Study Figure 7.1 on page 84 carefully:

- what do you think were the main features which caused the bridge to collapse when the earthquake occurred?

Most of the newer Californian bridges and buildings have foundations that are resistant to earthquakes. New high-rise buildings are supported by piles driven 50 m into the ground. They are also built with steel framing and designed to bend and flex safely in an earthquake.

ACTIVITY 3

Building safely

- Using materials such as straws, fine fuse wire and glue, construct frameworks of various heights and designs to support a 2 kg weight.
- Find out which is the strongest structure by standing each one on a bench and testing it with an artificial 'earthquake' – such as banging the bench.
- What problems did you encounter during the construction and testing?
- Write a report on your findings, recommending the most stable structure.

QUESTIONS ON CHAPTER 7

1 What is meant by an earthquake?

2 Why do earthquakes kill more people today than ever before?

3 How were most people killed in the Santa Cruz earthquake?

4 What caused this earthquake?

5 In your estimation where would the Santa Cruz earthquake fall on the Mercalli scale? What did the earthquake register on the Richter scale?

6 What are the main differences between the Mercalli and Richter scales?

7 Why does friction and 'jerky' movement along a fault cause more severe earthquakes?

8 Explain how seismic waves travel and how they can be used to 'look' at the Earth's structure.

9 You are working on the tsunami early warning station at Hawaii when you hear about the Alaskan earthquake. Use the information in Figure 7.8 (on page 91) to warn the New Zealanders, Mexicans and Peruvians – how long will it take for the waves to reach them?

10 A tsunami is about to arrive and you have to advise a ship's captain of the safest place for his ship – would you tell him to shelter in a port or in the open ocean? Give your reasons.

11 What happened in the town of Yungay in Peru in 1970?

12 Describe some of the safer ways to build to lessen the danger from earthquakes.

Solution to problem on p. 86

1995 − 1857 = 138 years
138 × 5.5 cm = 759 cm = 7.59 metres.

8

CONTINENTAL DRIFT AND PLATE MOVEMENTS

In 1620, Francis Bacon noticed that the coastlines of the landmasses on either side of the Atlantic appeared to match, but it was not until 1915 that scientists began to discuss the idea that continents could actually slowly move about on the Earth's surface. Alfred Wegener proposed the idea of 'continental drift'. He pointed out that certain continents could be refitted in a certain way so that matching coastlines and rock structures came together again. He started to collect evidence for the drifting apart of continents. He noticed that parts of the southern continents had been covered in ice-sheets at the same time, about 300 million years ago. Other clues came from fossils of the amphibious reptile *Mesosaurus* (see Figure 8.1) and from leaves of the plant *Glossopteris*, found in rocks of the same age in the southern continents on both sides of the ocean.

Figure 8.1 Cast of the fossil remains of *Mesosaurus*, found only in rocks 200 million years old in Brazil and South Africa

Jigsaw continents

- Trace the outlines of the main landmasses from a world atlas map on to thin card.
- Find out how well they fit together.

What evidence is there?

Figure 8.2 shows the outlines of two continents at a depth of 200 m rather than at the sea-level coastline. This is the top edge of the continental slope.

Figure 8.2 Were these continents once joined together?

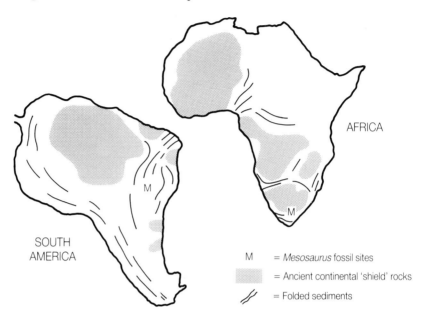

SOUTH AMERICA

AFRICA

M = *Mesosaurus* fossil sites

= Ancient continental 'shield' rocks

= Folded sediments

1) Trace the outlines and find out how well they fit.

2) Does a 'fit' at this level produce a better fit than at the coastline?

3) Wegener believed these two continents were once one landmass – do you agree?

4) Why do you think that no-one in Francis Bacon's day attempted to explain the matching coastline pattern that he observed?

5) Make a list of all the evidence you have so far to support Wegener's theory.

6) Figure 8.3 (overleaf) shows four maps that help to explain Wegener's theory. They show what the world looked like at four different times over the last 200 million years. Describe how the Americas have moved relative to Africa and Europe.

7) To which continent was Australia once joined?

8) What has happened to India, as shown by these maps? Look at a physical world atlas map of northern India – what feature do you notice?

9) How do you think Wegener would have explained this feature?

Figure 8.3 How has the world changed?

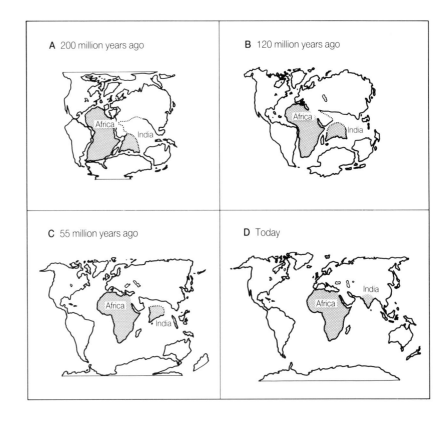

A 200 million years ago

B 120 million years ago

C 55 million years ago

D Today

Was Wegener right?

In 1915, most scientists thought Wegener's ideas were silly. They explained any sideways earth movements causing fold mountains in layered rocks as the Earth's skin wrinkling into folds as it cooled and contracted.

The truth is that although Wegener had a few strong clues, he had little real evidence to explain why or how the continents could move.

OCEAN RIDGES AND SEA-FLOOR SPREADING

In 1950, supporting evidence for drift came from the discovery of *ocean ridges*. Although these ridges are mainly below sea-level, they form the longest and largest mountain chains in the world. Scientists noticed that there was a lot of volcanic activity along the ridges. New ocean crust is forming from cooled lava, and from magma in intrusions. They noticed that the crust became steadily older at either side away from the ridges. It was suggested that the ocean floor on either side of a ridge is moving away, in a process called sea-floor spreading. This fresh evidence was good news at the time for scientists who believed in continental drift.

Figure 8.4 shows their *interpretation* of how the Atlantic
Ocean might have begun.

Figure 8.4 Sea-floor
spreading and
continental drift

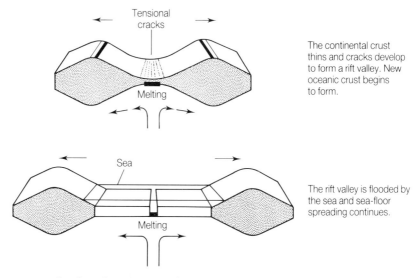

The continental crust
thins and cracks develop
to form a rift valley. New
oceanic crust begins
to form.

The rift valley is flooded by
the sea and sea-floor
spreading continues.

- Study the diagram and captions – then explain how two
  continents like South America and Africa could drift apart.

EXERCISE 2

Rates of movement

By the late 1960s, more accurate methods of measurement
meant that it became possible to find out that the Atlantic
Ocean is widening at a rate of 3 cm per year.

1) The northern Atlantic is now 6000 km wide – how much
   wider will it be in:
   (a) 100 years time;
   (b) 1000 years time?

2) Five hundred years ago, the Atlantic Ocean was crossed
   by Christopher Columbus – how wide was it then?

3) When did the Atlantic Ocean first start to open?

4) What must be the age of the oldest Atlantic oceanic
   crust?

5) Record this age on your classroom time-scale, described
   in Chapter 1.

EVIDENCE IN THE ROCKS

Some of the rocks in continents are very old. The age of the
oldest rock found so far is 3800 million years. This age
contrasts with the age of the ocean floor – there is no oceanic
crust older than 220 million years. Oceanic crust is much
thinner than continental crust and is mainly made of basalt.

Active and inactive zones

Active and inactive (stable) zones were mentioned in Chapter 3, on page 35, and you might like to read that section again. Volcanoes, earthquakes and fold mountains all occur in the world's active zones.

1) Look carefully at the map below (Figure 8.5) of the world's fold mountains, which also shows the 'active zones', within which most of the world's earthquakes and volcanoes are found. Compare it to the world map of volcanoes (Figure 3.8) and the map of world earthquakes (Figure 7.3). Describe the patterns of distribution on each map.

Figure 8.5 The world's fold mountains and active zones

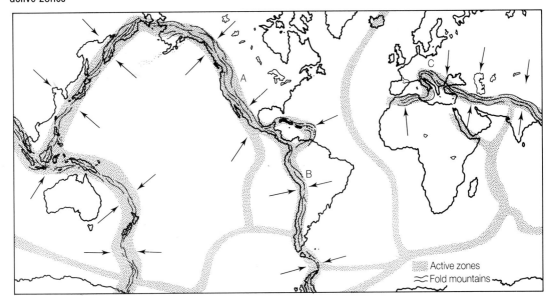

2) What patterns have all these maps in common?

3) What term is given to the very active parts of the Earth's surface?

4) What term is given to the relatively quiet zones where there are no volcanoes, earthquakes and fold mountains?

PLATE MOVEMENTS

By the late 1960s, with the new evidence about sea-floor spreading, scientists began to think differently about the active and inactive zones. The parts of the crust that were stable and rigid were thought of as units called 'plates'. Each plate moves against another plate, thereby causing earthquakes, volcanoes and fold mountains at its edges. Each plate is a rigid slab of rock. Plates are about 70 km thick under the oceans and up to 150 km thick under the continents. They are made of oceanic or continental crust, together with the top part of the mantle.

EXERCISE 4

Plates

1) Figure 8.6 shows the world's plates – how well do the plate boundaries match the pattern shown in Figure 8.5?

Figure 8.6 The world's plates

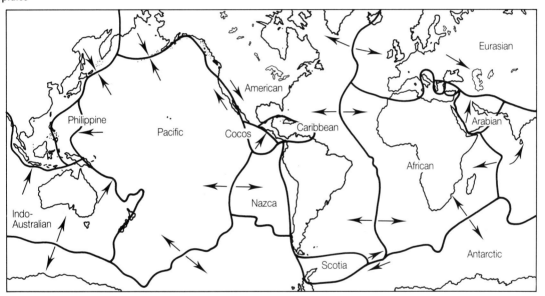

2) Name the world's six largest plates – which is the largest plate of all?

3) Name two examples of plates which are entirely surfaced with oceanic crust.

4) What plate is the British Isles part of?

5) Find Iceland in an atlas. It is positioned where the mid-Atlantic ridge rises above sea-level. What are the names of the two plates that make up the island?

WHY DO PLATES MOVE?

Plates are thought to move in response to heat flow inside the Earth. Scientists think that solid rocks deep in the mantle are able to flow slowly, rather like plasticine. There is thought to be an upward movement of hot plastic rocks in the mantle, as shown in Figure 8.7. The sideways movement below each plate is part of this convective movement and the overlying plate is dragged along as well. Eventually the flowing mantle rock cools and sinks, dragging oceanic crust down with it at ocean trenches. The continental crust cannot be dragged down into the mantle.

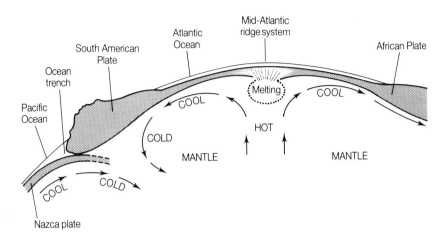

Figure 8.7 Convection currents in the mantle

PLATE MARGINS

The movements of plates mean that the Earth's surface is always changing. Some plates are growing in size at the expense of other plates that are slowly being destroyed. Continents drift apart, allowing oceans to form above the new oceanic crust between them. In other places, plates are moving together and the oceans between them are getting smaller. The arrows on the map (Figure 8.6) show that plates do not always move apart. Some are moving together, and some are just slipping past each other. There are three different kinds of plate boundary, as shown in Figure 8.8. Each type of plate margin has its own features.

Figure 8.8 The three kinds of plate margin

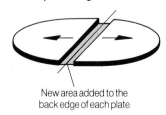

New area added to the back edge of each plate

CONSTRUCTIVE – plates move apart

Surface area of one plate is lost

DESTRUCTIVE – plates collide

Transform fault

CONSERVATIVE – plates slide past each other

Constructive margins

Where a convection current rises towards the surface, there is some melting of the top mantle rocks and magma forms. New igneous rocks are added to the oceanic plate. At ocean ridges the crust is being pulled apart and this causes cracks to develop, along which there is movement. These cracks are called *normal faults*. A rift valley develops when a wedge of crust sinks between two faults (see Figure 8.9). Other features of constructive margins are volcanic islands and sea-floor spreading.

Figure 8.9 The rift valley at an ocean ridge

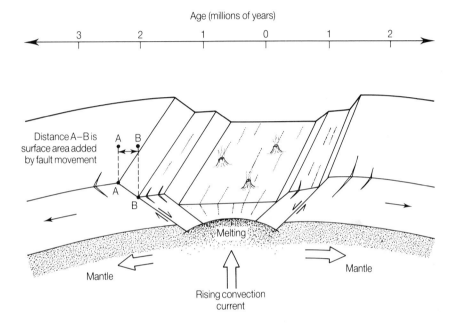

Destructive margins

This type of margin results from a collision of plates (see Figure 8.10 overleaf). Consider what happened to the piece of continental crust that is India. As India collided with Asia, the weaker oceanic crust sank below the continental crust, to become part of the mantle again. The layers of sediments on top of the oceanic plate were buckled and folded upwards, to be added to the continental landmass, so forming the Himalayan Mountains. This happened in the last 50–30 million years and it explains why it is possible to find fossils of sea shells in rocks on Mount Everest – 8840 m above sea-level. The exceptional height of the Himalayas is due to the double thickness of continental crust. In spite of erosion, uplift of the mountains continues. Figure 8.11 (overleaf) shows the effect of compression on rock layers.

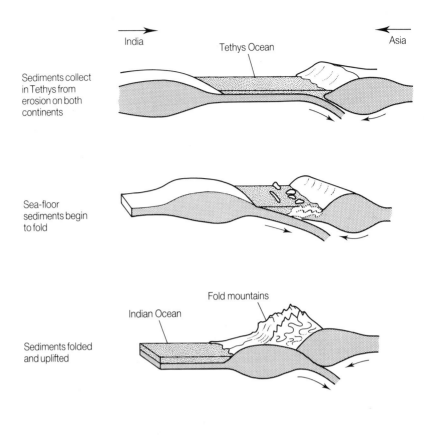

Figure 8.10 Collision of India and Asia to form the Himalayas

India   Tethys Ocean   Asia

Sediments collect in Tethys from erosion on both continents

Sea-floor sediments begin to fold

Fold mountains

Indian Ocean

Sediments folded and uplifted

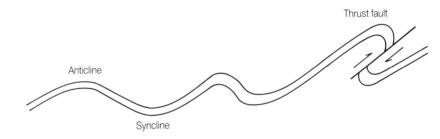

Figure 8.11 The compression of rock layers produces folding and faulting

Thrust fault

Anticline

Syncline

Fold mountains are forming along the west coast of South America where the Nazca plate is sinking beneath the continent. In this case, no second continent is involved but sediments are still scraped off the sinking plate and a deep *ocean trench* has formed where the Nazca plate is being dragged downwards.

Although the Pacific plate is large, it is losing surface area as it collides with the Asian plate to the west, producing deep ocean trenches. The frictional heat of the downward moving plate produces magma, which rises to form chains of volcanic islands known as *island arcs* (see Figure 8.12). Earthquakes are also very common events near destructive margins.

Figure 8.12 The formation of an island arc

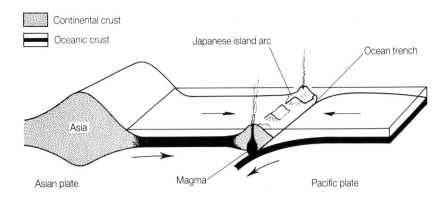

EXERCISE 5

Collision

1) Think about the effect of density differences to answer the following questions.
   (a) Why did part of the Indian plate sink under the Asian plate, rather than the other way round?
   (b) Why is it that sediments do not sink with the oceanic crust?
   (c) Why is it unlikely that any more of the Indian plate will sink beneath Asia?

2) Use an atlas to identify the fold mountain chains shown at A, B and C in Figure 8.5 on page 98.

3) What is the name given to:
   (a) a gentle upfold;
   (b) a downfold;
   (c) a fault caused by compression?

4) Draw a fourth diagram to add to Figure 8.10 on page 102 to predict how this situation will develop in the next 20 million years. Give reasons for your predictions.

5) Explain why ocean trenches are features which form where plates are colliding.

6) Use a good atlas to find out how deep the Marianas Trench is, and draw a scale diagram to compare it to normal ocean depth.

7) Look at an atlas map of south-east Asia and write down the names of two examples of island arcs.

Conservative margins

When two plates slip sideways along huge deep cracks called transform faults, surface area is neither lost nor gained. This type of plate boundary is called a conservative margin. The

San Andreas fault that runs through San Francisco, USA, is one example (see Figure 7.2 on page 85). At this type of boundary there are few volcanoes but many earthquakes. The devastating earthquakes are caused by sudden jerky movements along such faults.

EXERCISE 6

What next?

Since all the world's plates, with their continents, are still slowly moving, could you predict their positions in 20 million years time? Some plates will grow in size, and some will decrease as surface area is lost at destructive margins.

1) Look at the world map of plates (Figure 8.6) and summarise the information in a table with the headings:

   Name of plate   Will lose area   Will gain area

2) How will this affect the positions of the continents? (Working through Activity 2 below will help you to answer this question.)

ACTIVITY 2

Future plate movements

- Paste a copy of the world plate map on to thin card and allow it to dry, then cut out each plate.
- Place each plate in its correct position on a second copy of the plate map.
- Refer to the movement arrows shown in Figure 8.6 (on page 99) and slide each plate accordingly – overlap them where they collide.
- Compare the new positions of the continents and oceans to the map of today's positions.

PROBLEMS WITH THE PLATE THEORY

Although the idea of plates is better at explaining the facts than Wegener's continental drift ideas, no theory is perfect. One problem is that although most earthquakes, volcanoes and folds occur at plate edges, not all of them do so. For example, the biggest volcano in the world, in Hawaii, is in the middle of the Pacific plate. Large earthquakes still sometimes occur well away from plate edges. In time, the plate theory will probably change again, as more clues are found.

QUESTIONS ON CHAPTER 8

1 Write out and complete the following statements using the words listed.

> edges   central   6 cm   rift valley   convection
> Francis Bacon   fault   continental

(a) ___ noticed matching coastlines in 1620.

(b) Alfred Wegener's theory was called ___ drift.

(c) The plates move in response to ___ in the plastic mantle.

(d) Most earthquakes and volcanoes are at the ___ of plates. The ___ parts of plates are relatively inactive.

(e) A crack along which rocks move is called a ___.

(f) A ___ forms when a wedge of crust drops between two faults.

(g) The Atlantic Ocean is widening at about ___ per year.

2 Would you expect earthquakes to be more severe along ocean trenches or ridges? Give your reasons.

3 Three different kinds of fault are mentioned in this chapter – what is each type called and what sort of movement takes place along each?

4 What types of plate movement:
(a) add surface area;
(b) destroy surface area?

5 Explain how the sinking of one plate below another can lead to the creation of new land areas – what are the processes involved?

INDEX